EDUCATION & PHILOSOPHY

FORM 125 M

The Chicago Public Library

Received FEB 7 1985

from Contact to Contract

a teacher's employment guide

from Contact to Contract

a teacher's employment guide

by

REBECCA ANTHONY
and
GERALD ROE

43 Squantum St., Cranston, R. I. 02920

About the Authors –

REBECCA ANTHONY is Placement Associate in the Educational Placement Office at The University of Iowa. A graduate of Luther College, she holds a master's degree in counseling and human development from The University of Iowa and has had secondary teaching experience.

GERALD ROE is Associate Director of the Educational Placement Office at The University of Iowa. He holds a master's degree in education from the College of St. Thomas and has done additional graduate study in English at the University of Minnesota where he completed his undergraduate degree. He has prior teaching experience in public and private schools.

© Copyright 1982 by Rebecca Anthony and Gerald Roe

All rights reserved. No part of this book may be reproduced for inclusion in another publication of for any other commercial purpose without permission from the publisher.

Library of Congress Cataloging in Publication Data

Anthony, Rebecca, 1950 -
    From contact to contract.

    Bibliography: p.
    Includes index.
    1. Teachers – Selection and appointment. 2. Job hunting.
    I. Roe, Gerald. II. Title.
    LB2835.A57   1982   371.1'0023'73   82-17837
        ISBN 0-910328-37-4

Manufactured in the United States of America

(NOTE: The spot drawings appearing on random pages in this book were taken from *The Kindergarten Guide: An Illustrated Handbook Designed for the Self-Instruction of Kindergartners, Mothers, and Nurses,* by Maria Kraus-Boelte and John Kraus. Published by E. Steiger & Company, New York, 1892.)

For our parents —

Norman and Doris Jespersen

Fred and Maybell Roe

CONTENTS

Preface xi

Chapter One: **Preparing for Your Job Search** 1

        Increase your chances for success, 2
          Can I move?, 2
          Community Priority List, 3
          Can I teach more than one subject?, 4
          Can I work with students outside the classroom?, 4

Chapter Two: **The Resume** 6

        What is a resume and why do I need one?, 7
          Initial contacts, 7
          Interviews, 8
          Other uses, 8
        Preparing your resume, 8
          No single formula guarantees success, 8
          Information: classification and selection, 9
          Essentials, 9
          Options, 10
          Irrelevant items, 12
          Suggested headings for your resume, 13
          Suggested words for use in your resume, 14
          Novelty is not enough, 15
        Sample resumes, 16-20
        Resume Checklist, 22

CONTENTS — *Continued*

Chapter Three: **Letters** 23

    First impressions count, 23
    Outline for Standard Business Letter, 25
    Make your letter speak for you, 26
        What's in a name?, 26
        Aim for effect, 26
        Introduction, 27
        Request, 27
        Response, 27
    A single letter can affect your entire career, 28
    Letter of application, 28
        Sample, 29
    Letter of inquiry, 30
        Sample, 31
    Response letters, 32
        Sample, 33
    Sample letters, 35, 36
    Write each letter as if your career depends on it, 37
    Letter Checklist, 37

Chapter Four: **Forms and Records** 38

    Certification, 38
    Teacher Certification Offices in the U.S., 39-42
    Application forms, 43
        Sample, 44-48
        Equal Employment Opportunity: Applicant
          Data Form, 50
    Records, 51
    Sample Job Card, 52
    Sample Job Log, 53

CONTENTS — *Continued*

Chapter Five: **Interviews** 54

    An interview is a two-way street, 54
        Interview image, 55
        Interview process, 56
    Interviewer Appraisal Form, 58
    Interview settings, 59
    Interview preparation, 59
    Typical employer questions, 60
    Typical applicant questions, 61
    Irrelevant questions, 61
    Interview readiness, 62
    Content suggestions for interview portfolio, 63-64
    First impressions are lasting impressions, 65
    Interview closure, 66
    Interview Preparation Checklist, 66
    Evaluation and follow-up, 67
    Community Review: Needs and Expectations, 68-69

Chapter Six: **Contracts** 70

    Types of contracts, 70
    Sample teacher employment contract, 71
    Sample special service contract, 72
    Breaking a contract, 73-74
    Looking ahead, 74

Appendix 75

    Bibliography, 77-78
    Index, 79-80

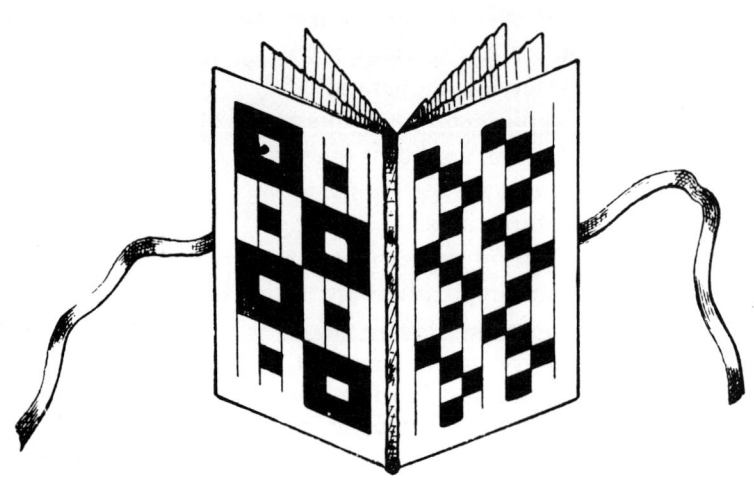

PREFACE

As associates in the Educational Placement Office at The University of Iowa we have assisted college students and new teachers beginning their job search; we have helped experienced teachers in relocating or rechanneling their careers; we have worked with teachers who for one reason or another are restricted to a specific geographic location; we have counseled unemployed teachers through the frustrations and disappointments of rejection; we have supported the underemployed but committed professionals determined to find employment which will permit full utilization of their talents and skills.

This book is written from a personal as well as a professional point of view. We both began our careers as classroom teachers. We know what it's like to organize and carry out a job search from our own experiences. We have drawn also on the experiences of our students and alumni, our colleagues in the College of Education here at The University of Iowa and in placement offices across the country, as well as employing officials in small rural school districts and huge metropolitan systems. We know that the job-seeking process is not nearly as mysterious or complex as it can appear.

The tools and techniques presented in this book apply to all teaching fields and to any market condition. It is a basic guide — complete, concise and specifically designed for educators. Individual chapters describe and illustrate each step of the employment process, from the initial contact to the final stage of accepting a contract.

REBECCA ANTHONY

GERALD ROE

Iowa City, Iowa
December, 1982

from
Contact
to
Contract

a teacher's
employment
guide

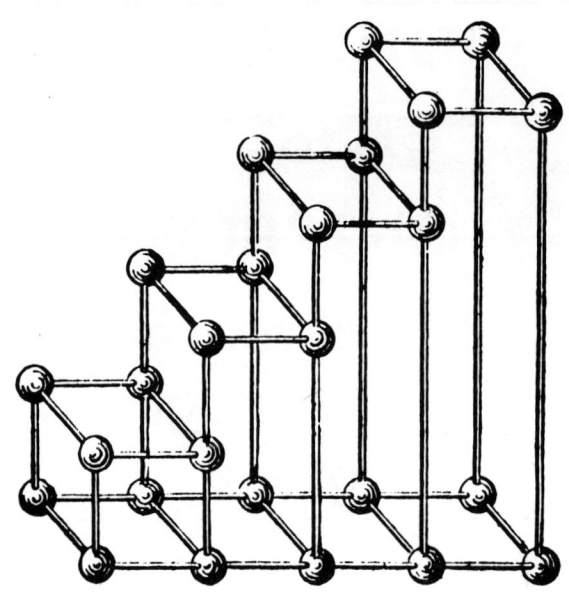

Chapter One

PREPARING FOR YOUR JOB SEARCH

Job seekers in education, whether new graduates or experienced professionals, share many of the same questions, apprehensions, and uncertainties about finding a suitable teaching position. The process by which teachers are selected may seem complex and mysterious. Those who receive contracts may be perceived as somehow luckier, having somehow been in just the right place at the right time to be hired. While luck can never be discounted, it is unwise to depend on good fortune. A clear understanding of each stage of the employment process will serve you far more reliably than any amount of luck. That's what this book is all about. Being hired is not the only measure of success. The best teachers, those who are most successful, are those who are hired for jobs that are right for them. That's what this book is about, too.

The job market in education is rarely constant, changes rapidly, and varies dramatically from time to time and from place to place. In the early '60's, teachers often had their pick of jobs and a teaching certificate could almost be considered an insurance policy against unemployment. Within a decade, the media were filled with reports of declining enrollments, budget restrictions, and the plight of the unemployed teacher. Regardless of enrollment trends or economic conditions, schools must be staffed. Regardless of the apparent job market, teaching positions become available as teachers leave the field through career change, retirement, illness, family responsibilities — even death. A tight job market does not mean that there are *no* jobs. Even in the worst of times, thousands of teachers are actually hired. Those who are hired, and especially those who are hired for jobs that are right for them, are those who have mastered the skills, processes, and techniques presented in this book. Skills, not secrets. Processes, not short-cuts. Techniques, not tricks.

This book is about the basics of the employment process in education. It has been designed to assist beginners as well as experienced professionals with every step of the job search — from making initial contacts with prospective employers through writing effective letters and resumes, completing application forms, and successful interviewing. Individual chapters are devoted to each aspect of the job search. The suggestions and examples presented will help the reader to understand each stage of the employment process, to acquire a working knowledge of common terms and to prepare the tools and utilize the techniques necessary for a successful job search.

Increase Your Chances For Success

The basis for success in your job search is an awareness of what you want to do and where you want to do it. Decisions concerning the direction of your job search should only be made after you have given careful thought to some important variables. Your chances for success can be enhanced by not limiting yourself too strictly at this point; it's easier to narrow the scope of your job search than it is to expand it. Give yourself as much latitude as you can and try to be as flexible as possible in considering the options open to you. Your success may well depend upon the commitment you make to following a few clearly defined steps. Recognize that your job search will be different from anyone else's because you are a unique individual with your own particular combination of skills, experiences, needs, and priorities. Consideration of the following questions can help you to focus or expand your job search and will also help you to estimate the amount of time, energy, and money that must be committed to achieving your goal.

Can I move?

One of the advantages of a career in education is that the profession is not limited to a specific geographic area or type of community. As an educator, you have literally thousands of locations to consider because nearly every community in the country has at least one school. While some people see this as a great opportunity, for others it can be a severely limiting factor. A number of potential teachers find it easier to return to or remain on home turf even at the risk of being unemployed or having to accept a job outside the profession until they can secure a teaching position.

Everyone knows that moving from a small town to a large urban area can be an exciting but frightening experience. Urbanites who move into very small communities face different but no less dramatic adjustments. Many people have successfully made the transition from one type of community to another. For those who are prepared to make the effort, each environment offers opportunities for developing comfortable and rewarding life styles. The census does not determine loneliness, nor does the availability of multiple resources ensure happiness. You probably will not spend your entire professional life in the same community. Your preferences and priorities may change as you progress in your career.

Finding your ideal community will require a little time and effort but the task can be made easier by developing and using a community priority list to determine your needs and those things most important to you. Your community priority list might look something like this:

Chapter One: Preparing for Your Job Search 3

COMMUNITY PRIORITY LIST

		HIGH PRIORITY	LOW PRIORITY
LOCATION:	Northeast	[ ]	[ ]
	Midwest	[ ]	[ ]
	Northwest	[ ]	[ ]
	Southeast	[ ]	[ ]
	Southwest	[ ]	[ ]
	Other (describe) _____		
TOPOGRAPHY:	Plains	[ ]	[ ]
	Mountains	[ ]	[ ]
	Seacoast	[ ]	[ ]
	Lakes	[ ]	[ ]
	Desert	[ ]	[ ]
	Describe Preferred Climate: _____		
COMMUNITY TYPE:	Inner City	[ ]	[ ]
	Suburban	[ ]	[ ]
	Medium Size	[ ]	[ ]
	Small Town	[ ]	[ ]
	Rural	[ ]	[ ]
COST OF LIVING:	Housing (Rental/Purchase)	[ ]	[ ]
	State Taxes (Income/Sales)	[ ]	[ ]
AFFILIATIONS:	Church	[ ]	[ ]
	Political & Service	[ ]	[ ]
	Professional Organizations	[ ]	[ ]
SERVICES:	Medical, Dental	[ ]	[ ]
	Public Transportation	[ ]	[ ]
	Mail Service	[ ]	[ ]
	Preschool, Day Care	[ ]	[ ]
	Continuing Education	[ ]	[ ]
	TV, Radio Stations	[ ]	[ ]
CONSUMER:	Shopping	[ ]	[ ]
	Banking	[ ]	[ ]
	Restaurants	[ ]	[ ]
	Auto/Home Repair	[ ]	[ ]
LEISURE:	Museums	[ ]	[ ]
	Libraries	[ ]	[ ]
	Fine Arts	[ ]	[ ]
	Health/Athletic Clubs	[ ]	[ ]
	Spectator Sports	[ ]	[ ]
	Parks	[ ]	[ ]
	Entertainment	[ ]	[ ]

Other Community Requirements: _____

_____

The priority list will not pinpoint a specific community for you, but it will help you to focus your job search. At a later time, you may use the priority list to evaluate a particular community where a job possibility exists. This tool can be useful in making decisions at any stage of your career; as your priorities and needs change, you will find it necessary to revise and possibly expand your list.

Can I teach more than one subject?

Most schools prefer to hire teachers in their major areas of preparation but a minor or second teaching area can be an asset. The need for a teacher who is prepared in more than one area may be due to a number of circumstances including the school's budget and curriculum, projected interest of the student body, the specific qualifications of the teacher being replaced, and the availability of qualified teachers. Some of these factors are more often associated with small schools, but even large districts may find it advantageous to hire teachers with dual certification. If your preparation did not include a teaching minor, but you have a significant number of hours in another discipline, you may check with the appropriate state department of public instruction to determine possibilities for certification.

Can I work with students outside the classroom?

Extracurricular activities play an important role in nearly every school. Sponsorship or coaching of such activities as a part of your professional responsibility will require a great deal of time and dedication. It may not always be pleasant to be in charge of an activity that meets at 6:30 a.m. or 8:30 p.m., but in most cases, the satisfaction gained far outweighs the time spent. You have a chance to meet students on a one-to-one basis, to explore common interests, to share special skills. Many times, because of classroom demands, this type of student-teacher relationship is only possible in extracurricular activities. You may volunteer for these responsibilities, but most school districts compensate faculty members for the time spent in coaching or sponsoring activities and events.

In keeping with contemporary emphasis on physical fitness and recreational activities, and in accordance with the guidelines established for the implementation of Title IX of the Educational Amendments Act of 1972, school districts have expanded opportunities for participation in organized, competitive sports. The effect of this rapid growth has been to provide many more opportunities for coaches at both elementary and secondary levels. Because only a few states have established certification requirements for coaching, it is often possible to serve as a coach if you can demonstrate to the employer your interest, preparation, and ability in a particular sport. A record of active participation in high school may be sufficient background for some programs; others may require collegiate experience. Keep in mind that very few new college graduates begin as head coaches. Most often, they begin at the assistant level.

Chapter One: Preparing for Your Job Search

Coaching is not limited to athletics. Other activities such as speech and drama clubs, chess clubs, photography clubs, cheerleading, and student government can provide opportunities for extracurricular involvement. If you wish to direct or assist with extracurricular activities, it is to your advantage to convey your interest and qualifications to a prospective employer.

After you have reached some preliminary decisions about the type of position and community which will be of interest to you, you will be ready to turn your attention to the basic steps of the hiring process. The following chapters, devoted to resumes, letters, applications, certification, interviews, and contracts will help you to understand employer expectations and procedures and to become aware of the steps you can take to increase your chances of finding the best teaching job for you.

Chapter Two

THE RESUME

OBJECTIVE	To secure an interview by conveying information which will stimulate employer interest.
FUNCTION	To accompany cover letter. To serve as a calling card. To facilitate an interview.
CONTENT	Educational background, training and course highlights. Related experience including volunteer work, honors, activities and awards. Additional information.
PREPARATION	Collect and organize material. Select categories. Write rough draft. Evaluate and revise. Get second opinion. Draft final copy.
APPEARANCE	Attractive layout with ample margins and suitable spacing. Free of grammatical and typographical errors. Visual effects and optional graphics.
PRODUCTION	Single page preferred. Standard size paper of good quality. Lithograph or best available photocopy.

Chapter Two: Resumes

What is a resume and why do I need one?

A resume is a concise and logically organized statement which effectively and efficiently conveys information concerning your specific qualifications, experiences, and interests. When you begin to apply for teaching positions, do not make the mistake of providing too little information to the employer. A letter indicating that you would like to be considered for a fifth-grade teaching position gives the employer insufficient information. On the other hand, if you attempt to provide all of the information an employer needs to assess your abilities and potential, the result will be a cumbersome letter of inordinate length which the employer may not take the time to read. Neither of these approaches — saying too little or too much — can succeed. The proper balance is best achieved by incorporating just the right amount of information into a resume which accompanies your letter.

The resume is not just for beginners. Experienced teachers, consultants, administrators, deans, and college presidents use the resume as a marketing technique. A beginning professional's resume will not be as extensive or complex as the experienced educator's, but the organization and appearance will require the same kind of careful attention to detail.

Beware of labels. Different forms of the resume have taken different names: *Vita,* Qualifications Summary, Data Sheet, *Curriculum Vitae,* Data Brief, Fact Sheet, Biography. Whole books have been written about the preparation and organization of these useful documents and fine distinctions between the various terms have been attempted. In most cases, such distinctions are unnecessary and confusing. All of the labels refer to one of the most effective tools you will use in your job search, a brief, organized statement of qualifications and experiences.

Preparation of a resume should be one of the initial steps in the job seeking process. Most teachers have had some experience with the other basic tools — business letters, application forms, even interviews. These more familiar items will be examined in subsequent chapters. The preparation and use of a resume will be presented first because the well-constructed resume can serve as the foundation of a successful job search and facilitate each step in the employment process.

Initial Contacts.

Always use a resume in initial contacts with employers. Enclose a copy of your resume with a letter of application for an announced position or with a letter inquiring about the availability of positions in your teaching field. In addition, you should be aware that you may use your resume in much the same way a business or calling card is used. If you visit a school district for the purpose of inquiring about available positions and/or obtaining an application form, leave a copy of your resume with the administrator with whom you speak. If you do not meet with an administrator, it is not necessary to leave a copy of your resume with the receptionist; enclose your resume when you return the completed application form. You may also encounter hiring officials either formally or informally at educational conferences, professional conventions, school functions or various other community-based events. In some situations, if you feel it is appropriate, you may leave your resume with the administrator. Use good judgment. If the situation is social or unrelated to your profession, plan to follow up this contact as soon as possible with a copy of your resume accompanied by a short letter reminding the administrator of your conversation.

Interviews

A resume may be very useful in the interview stage of the selection process. You may have the opportunity to interview with school district representatives who visit your campus. In most cases, your placement office will provide the recruiter with a copy of your placement file, but you should present your resume to the recruiter at the beginning of your interview. After initial contacts have been made and you have been invited to the school district for an interview, it is important to take several copies of your resume with you. The information contained in your resume can facilitate the interview and, if you are being interviewed by more than one person, it will be possible for each member of the selection committee to have at hand a summary of your qualifications.

Other Uses

Although the primary use of the resume is to convey information to prospective employers, you can use it in other ways. For example, the resume may be of assistance in collecting recommendations. When you request a reference from a faculty member, cooperating teacher, or administrator, your resume will permit them to write a statement which takes into account your present objective as well as past experience. The information contained in your resume will also be very useful to you as you complete application forms for individual schools. Try to develop the habit of revising and updating your resume as you gain experience. It will be to your advantage to have available a complete and accurate record of your professional career. A useful personal record, your resume can serve as a professional growth chart.

Preparing Your Resume

No Single Formula Guarantees Success

There is no magic formula for writing a resume. The resume you design may be quite different from anyone else's because it will reflect your individual personality, interests, qualifications, and goals. Before you even begin the process of gathering information to be used in preparing your resume, you should be aware that a well-constructed resume can tell the employer many things. In addition to conveying information about your qualifications and interests, the resume can demonstrate your language skills, organizational ability, and self-perception. Your choice of category headings, action words, and descriptive terms (discussed later in this section) can help to emphasize or highlight those aspects of your training and experience which you consider to be most significant. Much of this material may be contained in your college placement file and/or in the school's application form, but the resume permits you to arrange and prioritize the information in a manner you feel

Chapter Two: Resumes 9

best represents you as an individual. Relevant materials arranged in logical progression will assist the employer in comprehending and evaluating your qualifications. Although the length of the resume should be dictated by its content, most beginners should not exceed one page. When you consider the amount of material an administrator must examine before making decisions in the selection process, it is obvious that brevity is a virtue. Clarity and conciseness will be appreciated and will impress the employer with your ability to communicate effectively.

Information: Classification and Selection

The first step in preparing a resume involves identifying and selecting relevant items to be included. Considering the importance of the resume in your job search, allow sufficient time to review your experiences and activities, to evaluate their significance, and to classify them appropriately. Do not attempt to accomplish this task in one sitting; take the time to do a thorough job. If you rush through this stage, you are likely to overlook material which could make a significant contribution to your resume. Exercise care in selecting appropriate resume headings. The resume will be easier to construct and will be more interesting to read if the information is categorized properly.

Essentials

While there are very few hard and fast rules for resume preparation, it is possible to identify three categories that *must* be included in a professional educator's resume.

(1) Identification

The resume must clearly state your name, address, and telephone number. The name you use on your resume must be consistent with the name which will appear on other supporting documents, e.g., transcripts, placement file, and certificate. A discrepancy in the name appearing on one or more of the materials submitted may be confusing to the employer with the result that your application could be considered incomplete. Incomplete applications seldom receive full consideration. The address should be complete and without abbreviation; be sure to include Zip Code. If your present address is temporary, you should include a permanent address and telephone number, e.g., your parents' address. Telephone numbers should include Area Codes.

(2) Education

This section should include name and location of college(s) attended, dates of attendance, degree earned, and the date each degree was conferred. If you have attended many post-secondary institutions, it is permissible to list only the one granting the degree, if college activities, awards, etc., listed in other sections of the resume refer only to that institution. Name and location of your high school, including date diploma was granted, are optional.

(3) Relevant Experience

For beginning professionals, items to be included in this section are: student teaching and practicum experiences, part-time or summer paid employment, and volunteer work involving direct contact with school-age populations such as camp counseling, scout leadership, park and recreation activities supervision. Experienced teachers can omit student teaching unless the assignment was significantly different from the actual teaching experience. The resume should concentrate on professional employment and current related activities. Both beginners and experienced teachers should identify the experience in terms of responsibilities, name and location of employer, and dates of employment. (See sample resumes).

Options

In addition to the three essential items, any or all of the optional categories discussed in this section may be appropriate additions to your resume. The essentials must always be included, but the options can change as you progress in your career. Select only those which meet your needs.

Objective

An objective can be a useful item on your resume when you are seeking a well-defined position. Only one objective should be stated, and it should be concisely phrased and clearly focused. The objective should not be confused with long-range goals which are more appropriately discussed in an interview. If you have more than one objective, either in teaching or a related field, you should consider preparing two separate resumes.

Other Work

Most employers will be interested in your work experiences, even though they may not be directly related to your career. Work experiences should definitely be included if they account for gaps in your education or professional experience. It may not be necessary to list every work experience. Part-time and summer jobs could be summarized in a general statement such as: "To finance college expenses, I have held part-time and summer positions as cook, factory worker, usher, and bus driver from completion of high school to the present."

Areas of Knowledge

You may use a section of your resume to indicate to a prospective employer your competency and interest in a variety of educational areas such as multi-cultural education, developmental reading, individual education programs, extra-curricular activities, and coaching.

Educational Highlights

A selective list of college courses can emphasize and define your background in a major or minor area and reinforce your job objective. Complete course titles and numbers are not necessary; use brief descriptive titles.

Chapter Two: Resumes

Certification

Specific certification information regarding endorsements and approval areas issued by your state's department of public instruction can help to describe your qualifications to prospective employers.

Distinctions

Recognition of achievement in academic and extracurricular or civic activities may be presented in this category.

Memberships and College Activities

Memberships in professional associations, honorary societies, college, civic, or cultural organizations can illustrate your commitment to your profession and your college.

Publications/Presentations

Most beginners will have no need for this category; however, if you have published an article in a professional journal or have presented a paper at a professional conference, this information should be included.

Community Involvement

A record of participation in community activities and organizations can demonstrate your ability to work with people as well as your active interest in community affairs and willingness to share your time and talents.

Travel or Study Abroad

If you have studied abroad or traveled extensively, you may wish to list locations and dates. Most employers regard awareness of other cultures as an asset for any teacher regardless of grade level or subject specialty.

Language Competencies

In most cases, language competency is relevant only if you are truly fluent in another language. If you wish to be employed as a bilingual teacher, you should make this clear – possibly by including it in your career objective.

Avocations and Interests

Your leisure-time activities or hobbies may be related to school clubs, e.g., photography or ski clubs. In addition, the avocations may reflect something about your personality and help to present you as a well-rounded individual.

References

If you have references on file at your college placement office, you need only indicate the name, address and telephone number of the placement office from which references can be obtained. Individuals who have agreed to serve as references may be listed if you do not have a placement file.

Irrelevant

Anyone who has browsed through most of the literature dealing with job seeking or most collections of sample resumes, may find the items listed below so familiar as to seem required. While some of the items could have relevance to careers other than teaching, educators applying for jobs within the United States should never include these categories or this information in a resume.

Salary

In many cases, teachers' salaries are determined by a negotiating process and are a part of a master contract. Placement on the salary schedule is determined by educational level and years of experience.

Location and Ability to Travel

Your willingness to relocate can be assumed if you submit your resume (and cover letter) to a school district outside your immediate geographic area. Most positions in education do not require travel; in the rare instance where travel could be a requirement of the position, you can state your ability to travel in your cover letter and express this interest during the interview.

Date Available

Starting dates for positions in education are rarely negotiable. Your interest in an announced position implies that you will be available to begin employment at the appropriate time. If you are submitting a resume with a letter of inquiry, your letter may indicate that you are available immediately but would also like to be considered for future vacancies.

Personal

You're applying for a teaching position and you are a Caucasian with blonde hair and blue eyes, five feet tall weighing 98 pounds, thirty-two years old, a divorced mother of three, an active Presbyterian, born and raised in Grand Rapids, Michigan, in excellent health, and your Social Security Number is 478-62-1111. If you think this information does not have a great deal to do with your qualifications as an educator, you are absolutely correct. Many people are under the impression that this type of information is important to employers. Federal and state governments apparently think so too, because they have issued guidelines prohibiting employers from requiring much of this information prior to employment. Such items as race, sex, religion, ethnic background, national origin, and age can be discriminatory. Some states have instituted restrictions regarding the collection of this type of information whether or not it is offered voluntarily by the applicant. Regardless of state and federal guidelines, regardless of employer practices and preferences, this information is irrelevant to your qualifications as a professional educator and should not appear on your resume. Teachers applying for positions in foreign schools may include information regarding number of dependents or spouses' occupation since this information can be of importance in the selection process.

Chapter Two: Resumes

As you classify and arrange the material for your resume, remember that your goal is to convey information which will stimulate employer interest in your qualifications so that you will be invited to interview. Omit any items that are not directly related to your qualifications. Concentrate on the essentials and those options which will make a significant contribution to your resume.

Selection of appropriate headings is an important part of resume preparation. The following list of headings may be of assistance to you in the initial stages of constructing your resume. Study these suggestions, examine the sample resumes included in this chapter, and select or create the headings that will best call attention to your unique background and qualifications.

Suggested Headings for Your Resume

OBJECTIVE
JOB OBJECTIVE
TEACHING OBJECTIVE
CAREER OBJECTIVE
PROFESSIONAL OBJECTIVE
POSITION DESIRED

EDUCATION
EDUCATIONAL BACKGROUND
EDUCATIONAL PREPARATION
ACADEMIC BACKGROUND
ACADEMIC TRAINING

SPECIAL TRAINING
CERTIFICATION
ENDORSEMENTS

AREAS OF KNOWLEDGE
AREAS OF EXPERIENCE
AREAS OF EXPERTISE
EDUCATIONAL HIGHLIGHTS
COURSE HIGHLIGHTS
BACKGROUND HIGHLIGHTS
CAREER HIGHLIGHTS
PROFESSIONAL SKILLS

STUDENT TEACHING EXPERIENCE
PRACTICUM EXPERIENCE
TEACHING EXPERIENCE
COACHING EXPERIENCE
EXPERIENCE SUMMARY
EXPERIENCE HIGHLIGHTS
PROFESSIONAL BACKGROUND

ACHIEVEMENTS
CAREER ACHIEVEMENTS
EMPLOYMENT
OTHER WORK
ADDITIONAL EXPERIENCE

PART TIME & SUMMER WORK
    EXPERIENCE
VOLUNTEER ACTIVITIES
RELATED ACTIVITIES
CIVIC ACTIVITIES
PROFESSIONAL & COMMUNITY
    ACTIVITIES
COMMUNITY & OTHER ACTIVITIES

COLLEGE ACTIVITIES
ACTIVITIES & DISTINCTIONS
SPECIAL HONORS
COLLEGE DISTINCTIONS
HONORS & DISTINCTIONS
HONORS/AWARDS

MEMBERSHIPS
PROFESSIONAL MEMBERSHIPS
PROFESSIONAL AFFILIATIONS
PROFESSIONAL ORGANIZATIONS

SPECIAL TALENTS
LEISURE ACTIVITIES
SPECIAL SKILLS
INTERESTS
TRAVEL ABROAD
TRAVEL
LANGUAGE COMPETENCIES
MILITARY SERVICE

EXHIBITS
PUBLICATIONS
CURRENT RESEARCH INTERESTS
PRESENTATIONS
CONFERENCES ATTENDED

CREDENTIALS
PLACEMENT FILE
REFERENCES

Once you have selected headings for your resume, you will need to give careful attention to the words you choose to describe your activities and experiences. Make your resume come alive by choosing active verbs or "action words" and effective modifiers. Descriptive terms used appropriately and sparingly can demonstrate your awareness of and familiarity with a variety of educational programs and schedules. Avoid jargon and faddish language; terms familiar in one area of the country may be outdated or incomprehensible in another. The following examples may stimulate you to think of other dynamic and meaningful terms and expressions suited to your specific needs.

Suggested Words to Use in Your Resume

Action Words

accomplished
acquired
arranged
assisted
conducted
coordinated
created
designed
developed
directed
established
expanded
implemented
improved
initiated
instituted
introduced
maintained
managed
motivated
organized
originated
participated
planned
prepared
promoted
revised
scheduled
strengthened
supervised
trained

Modifiers

capable
consistent
effective
efficient
experienced
knowledgeable
proficient
qualified
successful

Descriptive Terms

open classroom
mainstreaming
resource room
behavior modification
residential setting
team teaching
self-contained
departmentalized
individual education plan
team planning
structured
non-structured
flexible scheduling
modular scheduling
learning centers
activity centers

Chapter Two: Resumes

Novelty Is Not Enough

There is no denying that creativity is an asset. The ability to formulate and develop an original idea into an attractive, eye-catching, informative resume that will stand out from all the others will unquestionably impress potential employers. Do not make the mistake of thinking this means you have to print your resume in purple ink on pink pebbled paper and fold it in a triangle. Gimmicks and whimsy are not required. Some readers will appreciate the novelty of a truly unusual presentation, some may be amused, and others may be offended by an approach which seems to them unprofessional and flippant.

The resume which represents you should be appropriate to a professional. In addition, if it is really going to represent you, it should be something you are comfortable with. If you are truly creative, don't shy away from using your talents. If you're not, don't despair. The resume does not have to be visually unique in order to be effective. Choose correctness over novelty.

Simple graphics used appropriately can help to make the resume visually interesting. Check with a local art supply store for transfer letters, designs or artwork which can be applied to the original copy of the resume before reproduction. (See sample resume on page 20.)

A note of caution. It is highly unlikely that you will require the services of a professional resume-writer. Most of the work in preparing a resume must be done by you. You may need the services of a typist, but there is probably little that a professional resume-writer could add at this stage of your career. Time delays as well as the cost of professional resume preparation must be considered. In addition, the packaged resume may appear too slick. You should be the person who makes the decisions regarding content and appearance of your resume. It is, after all, the first impression the employer will receive of you and it should be your own work.

The sample resumes on the next few pages are offered as guides, not models. They can be of assistance to you in formulating ideas about resume content, length, and layout. The variety of styles represented by the samples is only an indication of what can be done. You may find features in several resumes which are appealing. This can be the beginning point of creating your own individualized resume. As you review these samples, keep in mind the essential elements, the options, and the items considered irrelevant. Try to imagine yourself as the employer. Does the resume give you the information you require in order to make a decision?

TONY FRANCIS
418 Alcorn Street
St. Paul, Minnesota 55103
Telephone: (612) 354-1210

OBJECTIVE	Teacher: Elementary Education (K-8) or Reading (K-9)
AREAS OF KNOWLEDGE	Tutoring Individually Guided Education Team Teaching Developmental Reading Open Space Education Sports Activities, Coaching

EDUCATION	Hamline University, St. Paul, Minnesota — 4 years
	    B.S. Degree — May, 1982
	        Major: Elementary Education
	            Area of Specialization: Reading

EDUCATIONAL HIGHLIGHTS	Education Reading Clinic Educational Psychology (techniques & practicums) Creative Dramatics Psychology of Reading Children's Literature

STUDENT TEACHING	ADAMS ELEMENTARY, St. Paul, Minnesota 2/82-4/82
	
	Position: Student Teacher — 4th and 5th Grades
	
	Responsibilities:
	    Assist reading groups
	    Teach individualized math
	    Team teach social studies and language arts
	    Develop learning centers
	
	COMO PARK ELEMENTARY, St. Paul, Minn. 9/81-12/81
	
	Position: Student Teacher — Reading Clinic, 2nd Grade
	
	Responsibilities:
	    Organize curriculum materials
	    Teach reading to group of five students
	    Design and maintain progress charts

RELATED ACTIVITIES	Volunteer Tutor, St. Paul, Minnesota, summer of 1980 Umpire, Little League, St. Paul, Minnesota, summers, 1977-1981
CREDENTIALS ON FILE	Career Planning and Placement Hamline University Hewitt Avenue & Snelling Avenue North St. Paul, Minnesota 55106 Telephone: (612) 641-2064

Chapter Two: Resumes

David R. Michaels
67 Leaf Avenue
Charlottesville, Virginia 22901
Phone: (804) 354-3202

CAREER OBJECTIVE

English instructor at secondary level. Desire position which would utilize speech and drama skills.

PROFESSIONAL EXPERIENCE

9/81 – Present
Charlottesville High School, Charlottesville, Virginia
Instructor for special reading course, 10th grade American Literature and Language class, upperclass Mass Communications, and team-teacher for elective speech course for juniors.
Work with individuals, small groups and large groups using a variety of teaching strategies. Also assist with play productions, forensics, and debate.

ACTIVITIES and INTERESTS

1978–81
Costume and scenery construction, University productions
Virginia Players Repertory Company
Charlottesville Community Theatre, various minor roles

PART-TIME and SUMMER WORK EXPERIENCE

1978–1980
Member of Usher Corps, Virginia Center for the Arts

1976, 1977 (summers)
Receptionist, Dr. J. A. Jensen, DDS, Cincinnati, Ohio

ACADEMIC TRAINING

1978–81
The University of Virginia, Charlottesville, Virginia
Bachelor of Arts Degree
English Major, Speech Minor

1977
University of Cincinnati, Cincinnati, Ohio
General Studies

PROFESSIONAL AFFILIATIONS

Pi Lambda Theta
Speech Communication Association
Virginia Communication Association
National Council of Teachers of English

REFERENCES

Will be furnished upon request

TASSIA NICHOLS

SCHOOL ADDRESS
1-E Hawkeye Court
Iowa City, Iowa 52240
(319) 351-9184

PERMANENT ADDRESS
1435 West Lake Avenue
Glenview, Illinois 60025
(312) 966-2001

EDUCATIONAL PREPARATION

Glenbrook High School, Glenview, Illinois 1974-1978
The University of Iowa, Iowa City, Iowa 1978-1982 B.A. Special Education
                                                                                   Elementary Education

STUDENT TEACHING EXPERIENCE

Special Education: Trainable mentally retarded, Wright School, Cedar Rapids, eight weeks, fall semester; worked with ten students who were six to eight years of age and represented a wide range of social, physical and intellectual functioning. The main emphasis was language development, socialization skills and self-help skills.

Special Education: Physically handicapped, University Hospital School, Iowa City, eight weeks, fall semester; worked with small groups of severely handicapped adolescents in the areas of reading, math and language arts.

Elementary Education: Harwood Elementary, Kansas City, Missouri, Cooperative Urban Teacher Education program, eight weeks, spring semester; worked with twenty students in a third grade self-contained classroom. Located in the inner-city, student population consisted of various socio-economic and racial backgrounds. Assisted in all areas of instruction — large group, small group and individualized.

PRACTICUM EXPERIENCES

Sophomore Practicum: University Hospital School — Individual work with a twelve-year old autistic child.
Junior Practicums: Longfellow Elementary, 5th grade — Individual work with three students in reading and math.
                    Penn Elementary — Small group work with five low ability readers.

VOLUNTEER and RELATED WORK EXPERIENCE

Volunteer work at Psychiatric Hospital in Childhood Autism Program; 1978 — present.
Systems Unlimited, Inc. (assisting physically handicapped girls in bathing, toileting and dressing). Iowa City, September — December, 1980.
Monroe Developmental Center, Cedar Rapids, Teacher Associate, summer, 1981.

COLLEGE DISTINCTIONS and MEMBERSHIPS

Dean's List and Honors Student, 1978-1981
Janet R. Zober Memorial Award Scholarship, 1981
Council for Exceptional Children, 1978-1982
Iowa City Free Environment Alliance, 1981

CREDENTIALS ON FILE

Educational Placement Office, N302 Lindquist Center
The University of Iowa, Iowa City, Iowa 52242
(319) 353-4365

Chapter Two: Resumes

STEPHEN F. JAMES
4829 Park Avenue Place
Metairre, Louisiana 70001
(504) 771-0008

Educational Preparation

Baylor University Waco, Texas	M.A., 1978	Major — Social studies education
Mankato State University Mankato, Minnesota	B.A., 1973	Major — Political science Minor — Science

Teaching Experience

Bonnabel High School, Metairre, Louisiana, 1973 —
Presently a member of an interdisciplinary environmental studies team. Initiated and developed this program in 1974; also teaching American politics and economics to juniors and seniors.

Coaching Experience

Head tennis coach, Bonnabel High School, 1975 —
Assistant cross-country coach, Bonnabel High School, fall season, 1977

Professional and Community Activities

Faculty Council Representative, Bonnabel High School, 1978
Member of Bonnabel social studies textbook review committee, 1976 —
ISEA, NEA
Committee member of City of Metairre Parks & Recreation Board, 1976 —
Member of Mississippi Wildlife Preservation Committee, 1975 —

College Activities

Mankato State University student body president, 1973
Graduated "Cum Laude"
Captain of Mankato State University tennis team (1972-73) and participant, 1969-73
Member of Citizens for Environmental Action, Mankato, Minnesota, 1970-73

Position Desired

Teaching environmental studies, political science and economics at the secondary level. Qualified and interested in coaching high school tennis.

Placement File

Available from Career Development Office, U.B. 348, Baylor University, Waco, Texas 76703 upon request. Telephone: (817) 755-7331

RESUME OF:

 NATALIE NORMAN

TEMPORARY ADDRESS: 121 Territorial Hall, University of Oregon
Eugene, Oregon 97403 (503) 686-0030

PERMANENT ADDRESS: 104 Kirkwood, Medford, Oregon 97501 (503) 721-3044

TEACHING OBJECTIVE: Kindergarten Teacher

EDUCATION: Bachelor of Science, Elementary Education, 1982
(Early Childhood specialization)
University of Oregon, Eugene, Oregon

STUDENT TEACHING: Meadow Lark Elementary School, Eugene, Oregon,
Spring 1982
Morning and afternoon kindergarten classes;
involved in instruction of 32 children, kindergarten
roundup and parent conferences

Eadeschool, Springfield, Oregon, Fall 1981
Private preschool for children aged 3 to 5 years
Responsible for language development and activity centers

EMPLOYMENT: Summer aide, ABC Daycare, Medford, Oregon, 1981
Counselor, Ocean View Camp, Brookings, Oregon,
1979 and 1980

HONORS and
DISTINCTIONS: Dean's List, 6 semesters
Officer, College of Education Student Advisory Committee

LEISURE ACTIVITIES: Dance, piano, aquatics, camping

CREDENTIALS on FILE: Career Planning & Placement Services
University of Oregon
Eugene, Oregon 97403
(503) 686-3235

Chapter Two: Resumes

Now that you have reviewed the sample resumes, it is time for you to prepare a draft of your own. After you have written, evaluated, and revised your rough draft, seek a second opinion. A career counselor, a colleague, a principal, or a faculty member can check for errors and may also make helpful suggestions regarding the content. A second opinion can be invaluable in showing you how your resume will be perceived by another reader. You may want to incorporate in your final draft some of the suggestions for changes or additions. As you consider revising your initial draft, keep in mind the essential, optional, and irrelevant materials discussed earlier in this chapter. Keep in mind, too, that the resume is yours and should reflect those things which you consider important.

You will need to consider cost, quality, and production time when you select the process by which your resume will be reproduced. Production decisions may be determined by the type of service available in your community. The type of final draft you prepare depends upon the method of production you select. If your resume will be professionally typeset, you need only give the printer a clean copy free of grammatical and spelling errors. Be sure to ask to see a proof before the production is started so that you can correct any errors the typesetter may have made. If your resume will be produced by one of the photo-offset or photocopy processes, your final draft must be typed on white bond paper with no errors. Use an electric typewriter with a good, black ribbon and clean type. Hiring a typist to prepare your final copy will be worth the expense if you do not have access to a good typewriter or if you are not a competent typist. For any of the photographic processes, your final draft is used as the master from which the copies will be produced. The resume should be reproduced on good quality bond paper in white or a neutral color. Mimeographed, dittoed, or carbon-copy resumes are not acceptable. Use the resume checklist on page 22 to evaluate the choices you have made before having multiple copies produced.

DON'T CARVE IT IN STONE

A resume is not a permanent record. Unlike your college transcript, which records forever the courses taken and credits earned, your resume is a document which changes as you do. You will find a resume useful throughout your career in education, but the resume you prepare as a seasoned professional may bear little resemblance to the one you created as a beginner. As you gain experience it will be easy to add items to the various categories of your resume. You should also be aware that careful evaluation needs to take place in order to revise the resume to eliminate those items which become outdated or irrelevant. As your interests change and develop with experience, so should your resume.

Just as it is important for you to obtain advice and opinions about writing your first resume, when the time comes for you to revise your resume you should consult current career literature and/or seek advice from a career counselor. Don't wait until you need your resume to make the necessary changes, additions, and revisions. It is a good professional practice to maintain a current resume at all times. It will serve as a record of your growth and development, a handy reference of your professional interests and activities, and, of course, will be of vital importance should you decide to seek a different position.

	RESUME CHECKLIST	

YES   *NO*

[ ]   [ ]   Have I covered the essentials — identification, education, relevant experience?

[ ]   [ ]   Have I carefully considered and selected optional categories?

[ ]   [ ]   Have I chosen action words to describe my qualifications and experience?

[ ]   [ ]   Is the content complete, current and pertinent to my job search?

[ ]   [ ]   Is my resume as short as it can be and as long as it needs to be?

[ ]   [ ]   Is my resume visually attractive, perfectly typed and free of errors in punctuation, grammar and spelling?

[ ]   [ ]   Have I selected good quality paper in white or a neutral color?

[ ]   [ ]   Will the information presented help me get the job I want?

[ ]   [ ]   Do I know how to use my resume to my advantage?

[ ]   [ ]   Do I feel comfortable with my finished product?

Chapter Three

LETTERS

Writing effective letters is essentially the same as planning and preparing research papers or oral presentations for a class. The same skills of analysis, organization, and expression are required. This chapter will introduce and discuss the various types of letters typically prepared during the job-seeking process. Do not be dismayed at the thought of writing a great number of letters each specifically tailored to a unique situation. Although it is true that each letter must be individually composed, certain elements of the letters will be similar. Common sense dictates that the same letter not be used in every situation, but it is comparatively easy to develop variations on a basic letter that has been carefully constructed. The time spent in planning and preparing the first letter will pay off later; most skills are sharpened and refined by repetition.

First Impressions Count

Think of your letter as if it were a preliminary interview with the employer. You wouldn't go to an interview without giving some thought and attention to your appearance and grooming, nor would you behave in an unprofessional manner. Letters are no different. Appearance, style, and format of the letter are just as important as grooming and demeanor for a personal interview. Remember that your letter will create an impression, just as behavior and appearance at an interview create positive or negative impressions. The content of the letter and the interview are certainly more important than the initial impression, but in order for the employer to be able to evaluate objectively the content of your letter, it is essential that the first impression be favorable.

Letters that create a favorable impression share certain fundamental characteristics. Effective letters are:

- **addressed to an individual**
- **clear, concise, purposeful**
- **personalized**
- **grammatically perfect**
- **professional in appearance**
- **individually typed (no multiple copies)**

Most employers expect to receive letters written in a standard business style. Sample letters included in this chapter illustrate three basic styles for business letters: block, semi-block, and full block. The important thing in selecting a style for your letters is to find one that you can type easily and with which you are comfortable. The outline on the next page illustrates a standard style for business letters.

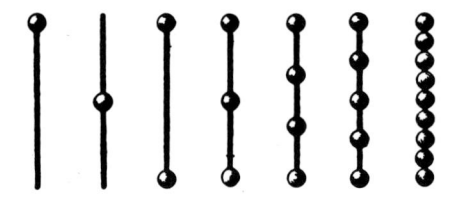

Chapter Three: Letters

(Outline for a Standard Business Letter)

                                                    Return Address *(Street or Box No.)*
                                                  City, State, Zip Code
                                                  Date

Inside Address *(Name, Title)*
Name of School District
Street Address
City, State, Zip Code

Salutation:

    Opening paragraph. _____

_____

_____

    Body of letter. *(May be more than one paragraph)* _____

_____

_____

    Concluding paragraph. _____

_____

_____

                                                  Complimentary closing,

                                                  (Signature)

                                                  Name Typed

Enc. *(If documents accompany letter)*

Make Your Letter Speak For You

The tone of your letter should be business-like but not stilted. Convey a courteous, positive, professional attitude in your letter as you would do in a face-to-face situation. Try to write as if you were speaking to the employer; let the tone and vocabulary of your letter represent your conversation at its best.

Selection of the stationery should be coordinated with the paper used for the resume and envelope. Choose white or neutral-colored paper of standard size and good quality. Post cards, memos, and decorated stationery are no more appropriate than flowery language or chatty cuteness.

What's in a Name?

If at all possible, address letters to specific individuals. We all prefer to see our name rather than "Occupant" on our mail. Names and titles of school officials can be found in state or national education directories. Letters may be addressed to the director of personnel or assistant superintendent for personnel; if you are unable to locate the name and title of a person responsible for personnel matters, it is appropriate to send your letter to the superintendent. If the directory indicates a title (Mr., Ms., Miss, Mrs., Dr.) before the person's name, use it. If no title is indicated, do not assume one. If only initials are given, or the name does not indicate gender, do not automatically address your correspondence to "Mr." However accustomed women administrators may be to such errors, the lack of perceptiveness on your part will not be appreciated.

In addition to the title used in the address, be conscious of the manner in which you write the salutation of the letter. Again, if a title has been indicated, use it exactly. If the name is ambiguous (or initials only are given) it is better to use the name in full or to use the official title along with the surname, e.g., "Dear E. B. Jones," or "Dear Superintendent Jones." In those cases where you are unable to locate the name or title of the person to whom your letter should be addressed, it is permissible to send a letter addressed only to the school district and to omit the salutation completely. Remember, however, that letters are generally more effective if they are addressed to an individual.

Aim for Effect

Although the letters you will write during your job search may have considerable variation, it is possible to identify three distinct purposes for your communication: *Introduction, Request, Response.* Most of the letters will have more than one purpose. Be sure that each purpose is conveyed to the reader clearly and without ambiguity.

Introduction

In the typical employment process, your first contact with an employer will be a letter of introduction. Employers may use the letter as the first step in the process of elimination; a sloppy or badly-constructed letter could mean that your application or inquiry will receive no further consideration. The ability to communicate effectively in writing is an important tool for any educator and employers expect that these skills have been mastered. A good letter will not only convey information to the employer but will also demonstrate your ability to communicate effectively. In addition to serving as an introduction, this letter can highlight or further develop items listed on the accompanying resume.

Request

Another purpose of writing to an employer may be to request information or action. Possible reasons for request letters may be:

to inquire about available positions

to obtain an application form

to schedule an interview appointment

to acquire curriculum and/or facility information

to determine status of application

to request clarification of information received

Most often, requests are included in letters of introduction or response.

Response

A letter of response is written to comply with an employer's directive or request, or to acknowledge personal contact. For example, a response letter accompanies a completed application form or other required documents sent to an employer. Other response letters may be written to accept or decline an interview invitation or contract offer or to express appreciation for interest or courtesy shown by the employer. Such a letter is *essential* after an interview.

A SINGLE LETTER CAN AFFECT YOUR ENTIRE CAREER

Letter of Application

Perhaps the most commonly used letter in the employment process is the letter of application. The application letter is appropriate only when a teaching position is definitely available. The vacancy may have been brought to your attention in any number of ways — a published advertisement in a newspaper or journal, an announcement through your college placement office, a direct communication from the school, or reliable "grape-vine" sources. (If you have heard of a position through the grapevine, try to get as much information as possible from your source. If information is limited, it may be best to send a letter of inquiry rather than a letter of application.)

The opening paragraph of the application letter should clearly indicate the purpose of the letter. The exact title of the position for which you are applying should be stated and it is customary to let the reader know how you learned of the position. A good first paragraph will assist the reader in comprehending the rest of the letter and will aid the employer in processing the communication efficiently. The opening sentences can vary with each letter; the necessity to communicate clearly in the initial paragraph does not mean that every letter must begin in the same fashion.

Use the body of the letter to refer to the enclosed resume and to expand upon or highlight educational experiences and background which are particularly related to the position as it has been described. Do not simply copy sections of your resume; use the letter to describe the experience more fully or to show how it relates to your qualifications for this particular job.

Additional possibilities for the body of the letter include information about a second teaching area, an academic specialty such as computer programming or data processing skills, remedial reading training or experience, creative writing, etc. Employers will also be interested in preparation for and willingness to assume responsibilities in athletic coaching, club sponsorship, forensics, or other extracurricular involvement.

In the concluding paragraph, some or all of the following items are appropriate. It is essential to indicate availability to interview with the district. If the school district is at some distance and your plans include visiting the area during a certain time period, e.g., spring vacation, include this information in the letter. Indicate that references and/or transcripts are being sent or are available upon request. If the application letter is the first communication with the prospective employer, request information about additional application procedures which may be required; if an application form has already been completed, enclose it with this letter.

(Sample Letter of Application)

67 Leaf Avenue
Charlottesville, Virginia 22901
March 1, 1982

Dr. Carroll Zelan, Superintendent
North City School District
49 Cove Avenue
Everett, Washington 98201

Dear Dr. Zelan:

The Placement Office at The University of Virginia–Charlottesville has notified me of a provisional one year opening in the English Department of the North City School District for the coming school year. Please consider me as an applicant for this position.

I received a Bachelor of Arts degree from The University of Virginia with a major in English and a minor in speech. My current teaching assignment includes teaching both elective and required English courses in grades 10-12. In addition, I assist with play productions and speech activities, an interest which I have pursued throughout high school and college.

The enclosed resume will give you more detailed information concerning my educational preparation and qualifications. My credentials are on file at the Placement Office and are being forwarded today.

I would welcome the opportunity to discuss this position in detail with you. I will be vacationing in the area over spring break, March 21-29, and could conveniently arrange a time to visit with you. Thank you for your consideration.

Sincerely,

David R. Michaels

Enc.

Letter of Inquiry

The letter of inquiry can be a useful tool for people who wish or need to restrict their job search to particular geographic locations. An inquiry letter may or may not be acknowledged by the district; practices vary depending upon the district's resources, needs, size, and popularity. It is common to receive a form letter in reply to a letter of inquiry; application forms may accompany the acknowledgement. Although the rate of response to inquiries may not be great, it is definitely worth the time and effort if a particular location is a necessity or of great interest. One vacancy is all you need to discover — then the application and interview may produce a job for you.

Unlike the typical letter of application, the letter of inquiry does not focus on a specific position. In a letter of inquiry, qualifications should be represented broadly; let the enclosed resume indicate specialties and specific qualifications. This letter is more concise and more general than the letter of application. Common sense and courtesy demand that this letter identify its purpose immediately. Employers are busy and will not appreciate irrelevant information or having to read the entire page to determine the request. For the district's convenience, and for a better chance of receiving a reply, enclose a stamped, self-addressed envelope.

The timing of a letter of inquiry may be of great importance if it is to receive serious consideration. For mid-year positions, late October to early November is probably the best time to send inquiries. Remember, it takes time to process letters, applications, and responses. For positions beginning in the fall, letters of inquiry may be sent after the beginning of the spring semester — February and March are perhaps the best months in which to send letters of inquiry. If an inquiry is sent too early or too late, it may not receive full consideration. Sending a letter of inquiry late in the summer is not likely to be productive since most hiring has been accomplished and there may not be sufficient time for the application process to be initiated and completed.

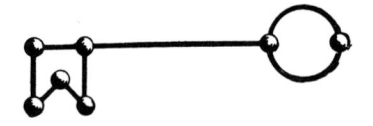

(Sample Letter of Inquiry)

1-E Hawkeye Court
Iowa City, Iowa 52240
March 24, 1982

Ms. Louise Johnson
Assistant Director of Personnel
Minneapolis Public Schools
807 N.E. Broadway
Minneapolis, Minnesota 55413

Dear Ms. Johnson:

I am writing to inquire if there will be fall teaching openings in the Minneapolis Public Schools for which I might be considered. I will receive my B.A. degree from The University of Iowa in May with a double major in elementary education (K-8) and special education (K-9).

As you will note from the enclosed resume, I have had experience with trainable mentally retarded children as well as physically handicapped students at the University Hospital School. Later this month, I will begin another eight-week full day student teaching experience in a self-contained third grade classroom at Harwood Elementary, Kansas City, Missouri. This experience with an inner city school is a part of the Cooperative Urban Teacher Education program.

My credentials, including references, are on file at The University of Iowa Educational Placement Office. If you anticipate vacancies in either elementary or special education, I would appreciate receiving an application form and information regarding your interviewing procedures. Thank you for your consideration.

Sincerely yours,

Tassia Nichols

Enc.

Response Letters

After the initial contact with an employer, there may be several reasons for additional written communication. In response to a request, a directive, or an offer from the employer, letters may be used to submit required materials, or to acknowledge a contract offer. Never send or return any document to an employer without a brief cover letter. The cover letter not only clarifies the reason for transmitting the document, but provides a record of what was sent, when, and to whom. Letters of response are typically used in the following situations.

(1) *To return application form*

A brief letter must accompany a completed application form. The letter should indicate compliance with specific instructions; for example, transcripts and references are being sent from your college. If you have not previously written a letter of application (perhaps because you visited the district office to obtain an application form), you will need to write a typical application letter and enclose a resume.

(2) *Accept/decline interview invitation*

As a result of your letter of application or an on-campus interview, you may be invited to an on-site interview where you will have the opportunity to meet other personnel involved in the hiring process, such as a building principal or department head, to tour the building where you will teach, and to learn more about the specific education programs of the district. Even if the offer was made in a telephone call from the employer, you should send a letter confirming the time and date of the interview; it is not necessary to send a letter if you decline the invitation to interview during the telephone conversation.

(3) *Follow-up to interview*

Within four or five days after an interview, you should send a follow-up letter to the interviewing official, either stating your continued interest or removing your name as a candidate for the position available. This brief letter is not only a matter of courtesy, but may influence the employer's decision. This letter can re-emphasize a particular aspect of your training or experience that relates to the position.

(Sample Follow-Up Letter)

418 Alcorn Street
St. Paul, Minnesota 55103
April 20, 1982

Mr. Robert Franker, Superintendent
School District 2
P.O. Box 237
Sheridan, Wyoming 82801

Dear Mr. Franker:

    It was a pleasure to visit with you on Friday concerning the reading opening at Lewis Elementary. I particularly appreciated the opportunity to have lunch with some of the faculty members at Lewis after meeting Ms. Larson, the principal.

    Sheridan's progressive approach to reading education through exploration and laboratory activities is impressive and challenging. Hamline's education programs, including reading clinic, practicums and student teaching experiences, have afforded me the opportunity to become familiar with a wide range of reading programs and curriculum materials. I feel that working with your staff would be a rewarding experience and I am confident that I could contribute to the development of your reading programs.

    As you requested, I will arrange to have an official transcript sent to your office. I look forward to hearing from you.

                                                      Sincerely,

                                                      Tony Francis

(4) *Accept/decline contract offer*

There are three ways in which contracts may be offered. The employer may offer a contract at the conclusion of the interview. This type of offer is likely to be made when a teacher is needed immediately to fill a vacant position, or when an on-site interview is not possible because of distance, e.g., foreign schools. Even if the offer is accepted and the contract signed in the employer's office, a letter indicating the date and location of your acceptance of the contract is advisable.

The employer may extend a contract offer by telephone. In some cases, you may state your intention to accept or decline an offer during the telephone conversation. Either decision should be immediately confirmed by letter. This will provide a written record of the action and will reinforce a verbal commitment.

In the event that a contract offer is received by mail without prior verbal notice, an immediate response is required. If you intend to accept the offer, a verbal commitment by telephone is appropriate. In addition, a written acceptance accompanies the signed contract when it is returned. If you decide to decline the offer, reply immediately expressing appreciation, but clearly stating that the offer will not be accepted.

In most cases, you may simply accept or decline a contract offer; however, it is possible that you will need some time to make a decision. If a contract offer has been received from one employer, but you anticipate receiving an offer from another school in which you are equally or even more interested, you must acknowledge the first offer, but a decision to accept or decline need not be indicated. Most contract offers will state a deadline for acceptance. If more time is needed to make a decision, you may request an extension of the deadline. If you make this request by telephone, you must confirm it with a letter. If the administrator does not grant an extension, you will have to make your decision within the allotted time. In any case, the employer must be informed of your decision as soon as possible. If the more desirable position is offered, a telephone call declining the contract offer should be made immediately to the first employer and, of course, a written confirmation is required.

Chapter Three: Letters

(Sample Contract Acceptance Letter)

                                                        4829 Park Avenue Place
                                                        Metairre, Louisiana 70001
                                                        May 5, 1982

Dr. Pete Harris, Director
Metro High School
141 State Street
St. Louis, Missouri 63121

Dear Dr. Harris:

I am pleased to accept your offer to teach environmental studies at Metro High School. I received the contract offer on May 2, and am enclosing the signed contract as you requested.

I look forward to joining your social studies staff and, as you mentioned during our telephone conversation of April 20, I will contact Dr. Herman concerning curriculum materials.

                                                                  Sincerely,

                                                              Stephen F. James

Enc.

(Sample Contract Rejection Letter)

                                                           4829 Park Avenue Place
                                                           Metairre, Louisiana 70001
                                                           May 3, 1982

Dr. Pete Harris, Director
Metro High School
141 State Street
St. Louis, Missouri 63121

Dear Dr. Harris:

I am returning the contract offer to teach at Metro High School which I received in the mail on April 30. On April 28, I verbally accepted a contract offer from another district for a position which includes duties as head tennis coach. Because of this commitment, I am unable to accept your offer.

Thank you for your consideration. I would like to express my appreciation for the courtesy extended to me during my interview at Metro High School.

                                                                          Sincerely,

                                                                     Stephen F. James

Enc.

Chapter Three: Letters

WRITE EACH LETTER AS IF YOUR CAREER DEPENDS UPON IT

The importance of letters to employers cannot be over-emphasized. Effective written communication is a part of an educator's professional responsibility; prompt, clear, concise communications are essential. Your letters will play a significant role in the success of your job search at any stage of your career. It is important for beginners and experienced teachers to remember that each letter has a purpose and an effect. The following checklist will be a helpful review of the essential elements of effective letters.

LETTER CHECKLIST

YES	NO	
[ ]	[ ]	Is my letter personalized (directed to a specific individual by correct name and title)?
[ ]	[ ]	Does my letter begin with a strong first statement?
[ ]	[ ]	Is the purpose of my letter clearly stated?
[ ]	[ ]	Is my letter concise and free of unnecessary jargon?
[ ]	[ ]	Does my letter reflect my personality as well as my qualifications?
[ ]	[ ]	Have I overused the personal pronoun "I"?
[ ]	[ ]	Have I checked for errors in grammar, spelling and punctuation?
[ ]	[ ]	Is my letter perfectly typed in a standard business format?
[ ]	[ ]	Does my letter require enclosures?
[ ]	[ ]	Do I have a copy for my records?

Chapter Four

FORMS AND RECORDS

The paper tools previously discussed — resumes and letters — provide the opportunity for originality and creativity emphasizing your unique background and abilities. This chapter will present a discussion of the more routine aspects of the job search — certification, application forms, and record-keeping. For many people, the word *routine* implies *dull* and there can be no doubt that job seekers at all levels have at times found these procedures frustrating, time-consuming, and boring. It may not be possible to make this aspect of the job search exciting and interesting; it can, however, be less painful if it is approached systematically with a sense of purpose and a clear understanding of what is expected.

Certification

A teaching certificate can be considered a license to work as an educator. The Department of Public Instruction in each state requires all public school teachers to obtain certification. In addition, many states require certification for educators in private and parochial schools.

It is necessary to apply for certification in the state in which you will teach. Many states have similar requirements for certification, but the teaching certificate does not transfer from one state to another. Departments of Public Instruction provide forms requesting specific information about the applicant's education and experience and may require college transcripts or other supporting documents. Most states also require a processing fee. The initial certificate is valid for a limited number of years and renewal may require additional education. State guidelines vary both in initial requirements and renewal policies.

Although a valid teaching certificate is a condition of employment, one need not wait to apply for positions until the certification process has been completed. Information available in academic libraries may answer preliminary questions about certification in other states. To inquire about certification possibilities, or to request application forms for certification, contact the appropriate state department of public instruction.

Chapter Four: Forms and Records 39

TEACHER CERTIFICATION OFFICES IN THE UNITED STATES

ALABAMA

Certification Section
State Department of Education
Room 349, State Office Building
501 Dexter Avenue
Montgomery, AL 36130
(205) 832-3130

ALASKA

Teacher Certification Office
State Department of Education
Pouch F, Alaska Office Building
Juneau, AK 99811
(907) 465-2831

ARIZONA

Certification Division
Arizona Department of Education
1535 West Jefferson
Phoenix, AZ 85007
(602) 255-4367

ARKANSAS

Teacher Education and Certification
Department of Education
State Capitol Mall
Little Rock, AR 72201
(501) 371-1474

CALIFORNIA

Commission for Teacher Preparation
  and Licensing
1020 "O" Street
Sacramento, CA 95814
(916) 445-7254

COLORADO

Division of Teacher Education and
  Certification
Colorado Department of Education
Room 310, State Office Building
201 East Colfax Avenue
Denver, CO 80203
(303) 839-3075

CONNECTICUT

Teacher Certification Unit
Connecticut Department of Education
P.O. Box 2219
Hartford, CT 06115
(203) 566-2670

DELAWARE

Certification and Personnel Division
State Department of Public
  Instruction
Townsend Building
Dover, DE 19901
(302) 678-4686

DISTRICT OF COLUMBIA

Board of Examiners
District of Columbia Public Schools
415 12th Street, N.W.
Washington, DC 20004
(202) 724-4279

FLORIDA

Teacher Education, Certification and
  Staff Development
Department of Education
Knott Building
Tallahassee, FL 32301
(904) 488-1234

GEORGIA

Teacher Certification
Georgia Department of Education
209 State Office Building
Atlanta, GA 30334
(404) 656-2604

HAWAII

Office of Personnel Services
State Department of Education
P.O. Box 2360
Honolulu, HI 96804
(808) 548-6384

IDAHO

Teacher Education and Certification
State Department of Education
Len Jordan Office Building
Boise, ID 83720
(208) 334-3475

ILLINOIS

Teacher Certification
Illinois Office of Education
100 North First Street
Springfield, IL 62777
(217) 782-2805

INDIANA

Teacher Education and Certification
Department of Public Instruction
Room 229, State House
Indianapolis, IN 46204
(317) 232-6636

IOWA

Teacher Education and Certification
  Division
Department of Public Instruction
Grimes State Office Building
Des Moines, IA 50319
(515) 281-3245

KANSAS

Accreditation and Certification
State Department of Education
Kansas State Education Building
120 East 10th Street
Topeka, KS 66612
(913) 296-2288

KENTUCKY

Council on Teacher Education
  and Certification
Kentucky Department of Education
1823 Capitol Plaza Tower
Frankfort, KY 40601
(502) 564-4606

LOUISIANA

Higher Education and Teacher
  Certification
State Department of Education
P.O. Box 44064
Baton Rouge, LA 70804
(504) 342-3490

MAINE

Department of Educational and
  Cultural Services
Division of Certification and Placement
Augusta, ME 04330
(207) 289-2441

MARYLAND

Division of Certification and
  Accreditation
Maryland Department of Education
P.O. Box 8717
Baltimore-Washington International
  Airport
Baltimore, MD 21240
(301) 659-2100

MASSACHUSETTS

Teacher Preparation, Certification and
  Placement Bureau
Massachusetts Department of
  Education
31 St. James Avenue
Boston, MA 02116
(617) 727-5726

MICHIGAN

Teacher Preparation and Certification
  Services
Michigan Department of Education
P.O. Box 30008
Lansing, MI 48909
(517) 373-3310

MINNESOTA

Personnel Licensing and Placement
Minnesota Department of Education
Capitol Square Building
550 Cedar Street
St. Paul, MN 55101
(612) 296-2046

MISSISSIPPI

Teacher Certification
State Department of Education
Sillers State Office Building, Suite 802
P.O. Box 771
Jackson, MS 39205
(601) 354-6869

Chapter Four: Forms and Records 41

MISSOURI

Teacher Education and Certification
Department of Elementary and
   Secondary Education
P.O. Box 480
State Department of Education
Jefferson City, MO 65102
(314) 751-3486

MONTANA

Certification and Teacher Education
Office of Public Instruction
1300 Eleventh Avenue
Helena, MT 59601
(406) 449-3150

NEBRASKA

Certification and Teacher Education
Nebraska State Department of
   Education
301 Centennial Mall, South
P.O. Box 94987
Lincoln, NE 68509
(402) 471-2496

NEVADA

Teacher Education and Certification
Nevada Department of Education
State Mail Room Complex
4045 S. Spencer, Suite A-47
Las Vegas, NV 89158
(702) 386-5277

NEW HAMPSHIRE

Teacher Education and Professional
   Standards
Department of Education
State House Annex
Concord, NH 03301
(603) 271-2407

NEW JERSEY

Teacher Education and Academic
   Credentials
New Jersey Department of Education
3535 Quakerbridge Road
P.O. Box 3181
Trenton, NJ 08619
(609) 292-4477

NEW MEXICO

Teacher Education and Certification
State Department of Education
Education Building
Santa Fe, NM 87503
(505) 827-2789

NEW YORK

Teacher Education and Certification
State Department of Education
Cultural Education Center
Nelson A. Rockefeller Empire State
   Plaza
Albany, NY 12230
(518) 474-6440

NORTH CAROLINA

Division of Teacher Education
   Standards and Certification
State Department of Public Instruction
Education Building
Raleigh, NC 27611
(919) 733-4125

NORTH DAKOTA

Certification
State Department of Public Instruction
State Capitol
Bismarck, ND 58505
(701) 224-2264

OHIO

Division of Teacher Education
   and Certification
State Department of Education
Ohio Departments Building,
   Room 1012
Columbus, OH 43215
(614) 466-3593

OKLAHOMA

Teacher Certification Section
State Department of Education
Oliver Hodge Memorial Education
   Building
Oklahoma City, OK 73105
(405) 521-3337

OREGON

Teacher Standards and Practices
　Commission
Oregon Department of Education
730 12th Street, S.E.
Salem, OR 97310
(503) 378-3586

PENNSYLVANIA

Bureau of Certification
Department of Education
Box 911, 333 Market Street
Harrisburg, PA 17108
(717) 783-6788

RHODE ISLAND

Teacher Education/Certification
Department of Education
199 Promenade Street
Providence, RI 02908
(401) 277-6836

SOUTH CAROLINA

Teacher Education and Certification
Department of Education
1015 Rutledge Building
1429 Senate Street
Columbia, SC 29201
(803) 758-5081

SOUTH DAKOTA

Teacher Certification
Division of Elementary and
　Secondary Education
Department of Education
Kneip Building
Pierre, SD 57501
(605) 773-3553

TENNESSEE

Teacher Education and Certification
State Department of Education
125 Cordell Hull Building
Nashville, TN 37219
(615) 741-1644

TEXAS

Teacher Certification
Texas Education Agency
201 East Eleventh Street
Austin, TX 78701
(512) 475-2721

UTAH

Certification
Utah State Board of Education
250 East Fifth South
Salt Lake City, UT 84111
(801) 533-5965

VERMONT

Teacher Certification Section
State Department of Education
Montpelier, VT 05602
(802) 828-3131

VIRGINIA

Teacher Certification
Department of Education
P.O. Box 60
Richmond, VA 23216
(804) 786-5300

WASHINGTON

Certification/Licensing
Office of the Superintendent of
　Public Instruction
Old Capitol Building
7510 Armstrong Street, SW, FG 11
Tumwater, WA 98504
(206) 753-6773

WEST VIRGINIA

Educational Personnel Certification
State Department of Education
Building 6, Capitol Complex
Charleston, WV 25305
(304) 348-7017

WISCONSIN

Teacher Certification
Bureau of Teacher Education and
　Certification
State Department of Public Instruction
125 South Webster Street
Madison, WI 53702
(608) 266-1027

WYOMING

Division of Certification,
　Placement and Teacher Education
State Department of Education
Cheyenne, WY 82002
(307) 777-7295

Application Forms

As a part of the application process, many schools will require that you submit, in addition to your letter and resume, a formal application blank. The application forms encountered during your job search will vary widely in content, length, and purpose. Do not be misled by the appearance of the blank. Some districts use a slick professional package to gather pre-employment information; others use a short, mimeographed form which may, at first glance, seem hastily prepared.

Regardless of the apparent usefulness of the form, it is a uniform method of obtaining relevant information from all applicants. Even though some application forms seem to serve only as a record of your interest in a teaching position, others may play a significant role in the selection process.

Make the Application Form Work for You

Be sure to follow instructions fully and complete all sections of the form. Use a typewriter unless specifically instructed to complete all or part of the form in your own handwriting. Do not leave blanks. If the information requested in any section of the form is not applicable to you, type a dash (–) or N/A (not applicable) in the space so that the reader knows that the item was not simply skipped or inadvertently omitted.

Even the simplest application form may be used as a screening device. Sloppy, illegible, incomplete applications can eliminate applicants from further consideration.

The application form is just as important as the letter and resume and will require the same kind of attention to detail. The physical appearance of the completed application is immediately apparent; neatness and accuracy are critical. Each part of the application can be a basis for evaluation whether you are merely filling in blanks or composing a response to an open-ended question. Typical open-ended questions might be: 'What is your philosophy of education?" or "Why do you want to work in this district?" Obviously, the content of your answers to such questions will be of importance — but it is not only the content which receives scrutiny. Your response may be evaluated on the basis of your ability to write complete sentences, to express your ideas clearly and logically, and to handle the mechanics of writing — spelling, grammar, punctuation, even handwriting may be considered.

Although the application forms vary in style, you can expect to encounter some or all of the items included in this sample.

(Sample Application Form)

POLK COUNTY SCHOOL DISTRICT
In the County of Polk, State of Wyoming

Application for Employment

PROFESSIONAL INTEREST

State position(s) and grade level desired in order of preference:

1. _____ 2. _____ 3. _____

List extracurricular activities you are willing to sponsor:

1. _____ 2. _____ 3. _____

IDENTIFICATION

Name _____
     First   *Middle Initial*   *Last*

Present Address _____
     Street   *City*

_____
     State   *Zip Code*   *Telephone*

Permanent Address _____
     Street   *City*

_____
     State   *Zip Code*   *Telephone*

Chapter Four: Forms and Records 45

EDUCATION

Undergraduate School: _____

Location: _____

    Date of Graduation: _____ Degree: _____

  Major: _____ Hours: _____

  Minor: _____ Hours: _____

Graduate School: _____

Location: _____

    Date of Graduation: _____ Degree: _____

  Major: _____ Hours: _____

  Minor: _____ Hours: _____

CERTIFICATION

Certificate(s) now held: _____ _____

If you do not have certification in this state, have you made application?

        Yes [ ]   No [ ]

PROFESSIONAL EXPERIENCE

List most recent experience first.   *(Beginning teachers indicate student teaching.)*

		Responsibilities (Grade level,
Dates	Name & Location of School	subjects taught)
_____	_____	_____
_____	_____	_____
_____	_____	_____

State total number of years of teaching experience: _____

OTHER WORK EXPERIENCE

Dates   Name & Address of Employer   Position Title & Duties

_____   _____   _____

_____   _____   _____

_____   _____   _____

_____   _____   _____

_____   _____   _____

College Activities:

Honors:

Professional activities & memberships:

Avocations:

Travel: *(Give dates & places.)*

REFERENCES

List three references who have first-hand knowledge of your scholarship and/or teaching ability.

       Name and Position   *Address*

1. _____

2. _____

3. _____

Place an asterisk by the name if reference is included in college placement file.

IN YOUR OWN HANDWRITING, respond to the following questions. Use only the space provided.

1. Why did you choose a career in education?

_____

_____

_____

_____

2. What strengths can you bring to our district and community?

_____

_____

_____

_____

_____

3. In addition to a standard curriculum, our district provides special opportunities for slow learners and for children with accelerated abilities. Do you have a preference for working with one of these three groups? Yes [ ]   No [ ]

WHY? _____

_____

_____

_____

GENERAL INFORMATION

It is the responsibility of the applicant to:

1. Submit completed application form
2. Forward college placement file or references
3. Provide college transcripts
4. Arrange a personal interview.

The information on this application form is a true and complete statement of my personal and professional record.

_____

Signature

_____

Date

Chapter Four: Forms and Records 49

Federal guidelines prohibit employers from requiring information regarding race, religion, or national origin. Various states have adopted guidelines prohibiting employers from requesting photographs or other types of information including date of birth, marital status, maiden name, and number of children. Some application forms contain questions which appear outdated, irrelevant, and possibly discriminatory. If the application contains questions concerning any of these items and you are uncertain of the legality of such questions, you may contact the state Equal Employment Opportunity Commission (EEOC) for clarification. In any case, you have three options:

(1) Complete the information as requested.

(2) Type a dash or N/A in the space.

(3) Indicate that the information will be provided upon employment.

To conform with state and federal reporting requirements, many districts have adopted a special form to collect data about their applicants. This form is often an insert which accompanies the application blank and the information requested will not enter into the selection process. A typical affirmative action form might be very similar to the sample on the next page.

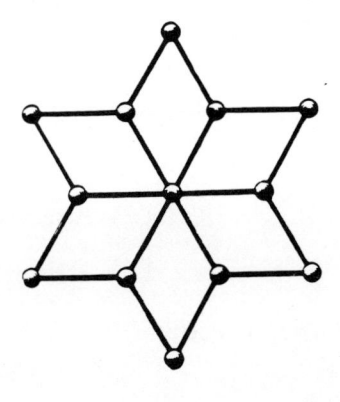

POLK COUNTY SCHOOL DISTRICT
In the County of Polk, State of Wyoming

Equal Employment Opportunity: Applicant Data Form

The completion of this form is voluntary; however, its completion will help our school comply with state and federal reporting requirements. The information will be used for statistical purposes only and will not in any way enter into the selection process. This form will not be filed with other application materials.

PRINT   Last Name   First Name   Middle Initial

Street Address

City   State   Zip Code

HANDICAP: YES [   ]   NO [   ]

A person handicapped but able to perform the job effectively; e.g., the blind, the deaf, the amputee, the paraplegic, the motor impaired, etc.

SEX: MALE [   ]   FEMALE [   ]   AGE: _____

ETHNIC BACKGROUND:

[   ] 1. White   [   ] 4. American Indian or Alaskan Native

[   ] 2. Black   [   ] 5. Asian or Pacific Islander

[   ] 3. Hispanic (Spanish origin or descent)

[   ] CHECK HERE IF YOU ARE A LEGAL RESIDENT OF THIS STATE
(Minimum of one year residence)

Chapter Four: Forms and Records

Be sure to proofread the completed application form and neatly correct any errors. Return the application form with a brief cover letter and a copy of your resume if it has not previously been submitted. If the application form calls for other supporting documents, indicate that they are enclosed or are being sent from the appropriate office (e.g., registrar's office, college placement office). Keep a copy of the application form for your personal file. It will be of assistance in completing application forms from other schools and certainly you will want to review it if you are invited to interview with the district.

Records

A common fault of most job seekers is the failure to organize and maintain accurate records. It is not essential to be an expert in organizational functions to develop a simple but effective system. The only investment needed may be a few inexpensive file folders or a three-ring notebook and some index cards. Whether you choose to work with file folders or with a notebook, keep a separate section for all correspondence with each school district contacted. Copies of letters of inquiry or application, copies of application forms and response letters, and any correspondence received from the district can be filed without much effort and will be available for easy reference at any time.

Not only will these copies be of assistance as you complete application forms for positions in other districts, they will be invaluable at the interview stage of the employment process. A review of the correspondence and application forms will help you to anticipate some of the topics that will be covered in the interview and may help you to formulate some questions about the district. Your responses to questions on the application form can be re-emphasized and reinforced during the personal interview.

In addition to maintaining correspondence files for each school, it will be helpful to develop a system which can very quickly provide an overall view of your job search. The following samples illustrate two possible formats for such a system. One or both may be used, and the record may be maintained on index cards or in a notebook or file folder.

Sample Job Card

EMPLOYER	MAILED	FOLLOW-UP	INTERVIEW	FOLLOW-UP LETTER	JOB OFFER OR REJECTION
Official: Title: Address: City/State: Date:	Letter & Resume Date_____ Credentials Date_____	Letter_____ Date_____ or Phone_____ Date_____ or Visit_____ Date_____ RESULTS:	Letter_____ TIME_____ OFFICIAL _____ _____ _____ _____ RESULTS:	Date_____	Date_____ RETURN THE CONTRACT Date_____
EMPLOYER School District 2 Official: Mr. Earl Gordon Title: Supt. Address: P.O. Box 237 City/State: Sheridan, WY 82801 Date:	**MAILED** Letter & Resume Date 3/5 Credentials Date 3/7	**FOLLOW-UP** Letter ✓ Date 4/2 or Phone_____ Date_____ or Visit_____ Date_____ RESULTS: Interview arranged	**INTERVIEW** Letter ✓ TIME 10 AM OFFICIAL Mr. Gordon and Karen Larsen Principal, Lewis Elem. RESULTS: Transcripts requested	**FOLLOW-UP LETTER** Date 4/20 Arranged to have transcripts sent	**JOB OFFER OR REJECTION** Date 5/6 RETURN THE CONTRACT Date 5/12 Accepted!

Arrange cards alphabetically by school system. Keep in small file box or notebook.

JOB LOG

Name and Address of School Administrator's Name & Title	Initial Contact (Letter and Resume or On-Campus Interview)	Follow-up to initial contact, credentials & transcript sent, application form returned.	Second Contact (on-site interview)	Follow-up to Second contact (Thank-you letter and community checklist)	Job Offer or Rejection	Accept or Decline Contract	NOTES

Chapter Five

INTERVIEWS

Earlier chapters have discussed the paper stages of the job search. The resume, the letters, the application forms all have one basic objective — to secure an interview. This chapter will discuss the direct personal encounter with an employing official that can make all of the previous work pay off.

An Interview Is a Two-Way Street

Many job seekers begin with the impression that the interview is a kind of examination. There is an element of truth in this conception but, by definition, an interview is a two-way process. The word interview comes into our language from the French *entrevoir* and the Latin *inter videre* and means, literally, "to see about each other." In a good interview, this is exactly what happens. The participants engage in a professional conversation for the purpose of exchanging information and impressions.

In any interview, the employing official will attempt to discover information related to four basic question. How will this applicant:

1. relate with students in this school?
2. work with other faculty members?
3. cooperate with the administration?
4. fit into this community?

As the interviewer attempts to answer these questions based upon the applicant's responses, behavior, and personality, the applicant should also seek answers to these same questions.

Some of the items the applicant may want to consider regarding the four basic questions might include:

(1) *How will I relate with students in this school?*

In order to answer this question, one needs information about the general academic level of the students. How many students are college-bound? What is the retention rate? What is the ethnic and economic background of the students? Are the students active in extra-curricular activities?

(2) *How will I work with other faculty members?*

How is the department structured? What is the role of the department chairperson? What type of curriculum guidelines are prescribed? What curriculum materials are available? Are consultants utilized? Is there opportunity for team teaching and team planning?

(3) *How will I cooperate with the administration?*

How does the principal view the administrator's role? What are the routine procedures for such items as attendance records, tardiness reports, lesson plans, etc.? What are the procedures and objectives for observation and evaluation?

(4) *How will I fit into this community?*

Does the community value and support education? Are there opportunities for community involvement? Will my values be accepted and fostered by the community?

Interview Image

Teacher selection may sometimes appear to be complex, mysterious, even arbitrary. In reality, the process is generally well defined and easily understood. Nearly every school district has a set of guidelines regarding characteristics or qualities desired and sought in new staff members. Whether or not the guidelines have been formally drawn up and adopted as a matter of policy, they do exist. Although guidelines vary from one district to another, the following qualities or characteristics are typical items for consideration:

Communication skills

Knowledge of the subject area

Enthusiasm

Empathy

Innovation/creativity

Personality

Social skills

Self esteem

Goals (personal and professional)

Appearance

Certification probability

Grade point average

In addition to these qualities and characteristics, administrators have other means of evaluating teacher applicants. Fairly or unfairly, body language and non-verbal cues such as those listed below may play a significant part in the selection process.

Clothing

Grooming

Facial expression

Eye contact

Voice

Posture

Hand shake

Smoking/gum chewing

Fidgeting

Nervous laughter

Perspiration

Non-verbal cues related to clothing and grooming are easy to control; you can plan to make a good appearance. Other non-verbal cues or body language can be influenced by tension and anxiety. Interviewers understand that an applicant may be nervous and most of them will attempt to make the candidate as comfortable as possible in order to facilitate a productive interview. The applicant must also contribute to a comfortable atmosphere by attempting to control visible signs of nervousness. Most people can greatly suppress or even overcome the outward signs of anxiety by focusing on the other person. Try to concentrate on what the interviewer is saying rather than worrying about your hands or feet.

The Interview Process

One of the things that makes job seeking so interesting and exciting is the variety of interview situations and personnel encountered. In the simplest interview situation, the applicant may meet and talk with one person who is solely responsible for every aspect of the hiring process. More commonly, additional people will be involved. An initial interview may be conducted by a personnel administrator, followed by a meeting with the building principal and in some cases, a further conversation with a curriculum coordinator, department chair, other teachers who comprise a selection committee, school board members — possibly even a student committee. Time allotted for an interview may range from thirty minutes to several hours.

Some school districts use a highly structured format for preliminary or screening interviews. A uniform set of questions may be asked of each applicant and the applicant's responses recorded either on a standardized form completed by the interviewer or on tape for subsequent evaluation. The interviewer may use a system which does not allow for interchange between the two parties; in these cases, the interviewer refrains from registering approval or disapproval of an applicant's response and will not interpret or expand upon a question, although the question may be repeated.

A less obvious format may also be employed for structured interviews. The interviewer may ask the same questions of each applicant, but without the use of a standardized form or a tape recorder. A skilled professional may conduct a highly structured interview while giving the appearance of leading a casual conversation.

Some interviewers prefer to work in a less structured fashion. The unstructured interview may allow more opportunity for the applicant to exercise some control over the direction of the conversation. Typically, an unstructured interview may rely more heavily on open-ended questions providing opportunity for more interchange between the participants. The interviewer may pick up on some part of the applicant's response to a particular question and explore one topic more deeply. Certain hiring officials prefer this approach because it places greater responsibility on the applicant. A skilled interviewer can use this approach effectively and still allow sufficient time to cover the essentials according to established guidelines. The applicant must be sensitive to the amount of time devoted to each response, using good judgment in order not to dominate the conversation but, if necessary, to keep it moving and to change the focus.

It is essential to approach an interview with some clear idea of information to be conveyed to the employer about yourself and your abilities and experiences as well as some questions about the position, the district and the community. As the interview progresses, keep a mental checklist to ensure that consideration is given to these points. It is especially important to keep a mental checklist in the event the interviewer is inexperienced, unskilled, or uncomfortable in an interview situation. Most personnel administrators are highly skilled and proficient; principals, superintendents, or other support personnel may not have the expertise to conduct efficient, productive interviews.

During the selection process, an applicant is likely to encounter both structured and unstructured situations; the structured interview is most commonly used in initial screening, and a less structured approach is more likely to be used in the actual selection stage. Most interviewers employ a combination of the structured and unstructured techniques in order to individualize the interview and ensure flexibility. Employers may rely on mental notes during the interview, but many of them will transfer their thoughts into written form at the earliest opportunity. An appraisal form something like the following is often used in order to record evaluations in a consistent manner.

INTERVIEWER APPRAISAL FORM

Interviewer_____ **Date**_____ **College**_____

Candidate's Name_____ **Major**_____ **Minor**_____

CHARACTERISTICS   **EVALUATION**

	Outstanding	Above Average	Acceptable	Marginal
Appearance and Grooming				

Preparations for Interview
    Knowledge of subject area
    Knowledge of profession				

Communication Skills
    Vocabulary
    Voice
    Confidence				

Maturity				
Creativity				

Personality
    Enthusiasm
    Sincerity
    Sense of humor				

Overall Qualifications
    Academic preparation
    Apparent intelligence
    General attitude				

Outside Interests
    Coaching
    Other_____				

Overall Evaluation
    Long range potential
    Drive and ambition				

Comments:_____

_____

_____ Office Invitation _____ Uncertain _____ No Interest

Interview Settings

Representatives of school districts frequently visit college campuses for the purpose of conducting screening interviews. Because recruiters often see a dozen or more applicants in a single day's on-campus visit, some type of structure is essential. Most employers use on-campus recruiting as a preliminary step in the employment process. Applicants may subsequently be invited to the school district for a more extensive and comprehensive interview. For potential teachers, on-campus interviews represent an inexpensive and effective method of talking with a variety of employers. The on-campus interview offers applicants a good introduction to interviewing in a familiar, non-threatening environment.

An "on-site" interview, one that is held at the school district, is generally a requirement before a contract can be offered. On-site interviews may be arranged in several ways. The school district may invite the applicant as a result of a letter of application, resume, and completed application form, as a result of an on-campus interview, or as the result of the applicant's request for an interview. In contrast to the on-campus interviews, which are usually designed for screening purposes, the on-site interview focuses more on selection. Consequently, the applicant usually meets with several people involved in the selection process, has an opportunity to tour the facilities, and to become familiar with the community in which the district is located.

In addition to on-campus and on-site interviews, there are other possibilities. Because of distance, employers may arrange interviews in settings such as hotels, airport lobbies, and restaurants. Regardless of the setting, remember that the interview is a serious matter – not just a casual conversation. It can be informal, friendly, very cordial – but an interview is an important professional conversation with long-term effects. It is essential, therefore, to take steps to ensure adequate preparation for the interview.

Interview Preparation

In spite of the importance of the interview, employers are amazed at the number of candidates who approach the interview without apparent preparation. Interview preparation need not be a difficult task, but it will be time consuming. Do not wait until you are driving to the interview to get your thoughts in order. You expect the person conducting the interview to have reviewed your letter, resume, application, and credentials in order to learn something about you. In addition, you expect the interviewer to be able to provide you with information about the position, the school district, and the community.

It is only reasonable that the employer has similar expectations of you. You can be expected to have some knowledge of the school district and community. You can be expected to articulate your thoughts about educational philosophy, curriculum development, and your general knowledge of school operations. You can be expected to describe concisely and with some insight your educational preparation, your classroom experiences, and related activities. You can be expected to have given some thought to who you are, why you are in education, and what you want to do in the future.

Large questions such as these are not as remote, difficult, and forbidding as they may seem. You have been accumulating your answers to these questions for a long time. A little effort will help you to organize your thoughts and to formulate clear, intelligent responses to these questions, and to arrive at a few questions of your own.

TYPICAL EMPLOYER QUESTIONS

Why did you decide on a career in education?

Tell me something about your background.

What is your philosophy of education?

Tell me about your student teaching experience.

How was your room organized? What was the atmosphere of your room? What was the socio-economic level of your students?

As you look back on your teaching experience, what was most effective about you? About your style? What was least effective about your teaching style?

What worked best for you in classroom control?

How do you provide for individual differences within your classroom?

How can you get students excited about your subject area?

What innovative ideas would you like to initiate in your classroom?

What strategies and/or materials would you use to aid students in developing creativity?

Name three effective ways to motivate students.

What kind of relationship do you want with your students?

In planning your lessons or units of study, how do you organize and prepare your material?

What do you anticipate as being the most satisfying aspect of teaching?

What do you anticipate as being the least satisfying aspect of teaching?

What hobbies and/or interests do you have that might help you as a teacher in the classroom?

Chapter Five: Interviews 61

With what extracurricular activities would you be willing to assist?

What are your professional plans?

What have you read in the last six months or year?

If you could spend a day doing anything you wanted, what would you do?

TYPICAL APPLICANT QUESTIONS

Are extracurricular assignments available for teachers interested and qualified in after school activities?

How many students participate in extracurricular activities?

Does your district offer faculty inservice training days during the school year?

What reading series do you use in upper grades?

In the past few years what has been the average faculty turnover rate?

Is there a budget established for supplies which need to be purchased during the school year?

Do you have an active teacher-parent organization?

What percentage of your graduates continue their education?

What is the retention rate for secondary students?

Are there opportunities for team teaching or team planning?

What types of support personnel are employed by this district, e.g., consultants, coordinators, counselors, etc.?

Who is responsible for the instruction in the use of resource materials in your library or learning center?

Irrelevant Questions

In addition to questions such as those presented above, some consideration should be given to the possibility of encountering irrelevant and possibly discriminatory questions. The same state and federal guidelines which proscribe certain questions on application materials apply in interview situations. Any interviewer who asks for information regarding race, religion or national origin is in violation of federal law. Interviewers are also obligated to follow state guidelines which may prohibit questions dealing with other potentially discriminatory information. Examples of such questions might be:

What is your marital status?

What was your maiden name?

Do you have children or do you anticipate starting a family?

Who cares for your children?

What is your father's occupation?

What is your native language?

Have you ever been arrested?

Do you own your home?

What church do you attend?

What is your date of birth? Where were you born?

What is the lowest salary you will accept?

In responding to this type of question an applicant has basically the same three options as in completing an application form: (1) give the information as requested; (2) indicate that the information is not applicable or relevant; (3) indicate that the information will be provided upon employment.

In preparation for interviews, it is essential that you give some thought to the manner in which you might respond to questions such as these. Your answers may vary depending upon the situation. For example, if you sense that the interviewer is merely trying to make you comfortable by engaging in small talk about your family, you may respond differently than if you suspect that the question is intended to be discriminatory. Whether or not you feel that the question is discriminatory in nature, you may firmly but tactfully decline to answer. If you choose to answer, let the interviewer know that you do not consider the question relevant to your qualifications. For example, you might respond to a question about marital status by saying, "I'm not sure how this relates to my work as a third-grade teacher, but I am married." Remember, however, that you are not obligated to answer such a question and do not be intimidated by the interviewer's questions. If you have prepared adequately and have decided in advance how you will respond to irrelevant or discriminatory questions, you should have the confidence to respond clearly and without hesitation or embarrassment.

Interview Readiness

In preparation for an interview, it is essential to collect and organize material in a convenient and useable fashion. An interview portfolio containing materials that are not usually a part of a resume or credentials can be used effectively. A portfolio is not to be given to the employer but should be used to present materials that can strengthen a verbal response or demonstrate a skill or talent. In some situations, a portfolio may not be necessary or even appropriate. It is important to be perceptive in how and when to use the materials to your advantage.

Content Suggestions for Interview Portfolio

Transcript. In the event the employer should inquire about your course work or grade point average, a copy of the transcript can provide immediate and accurate information. The portfolio may contain one copy of an official transcript along with several photocopies which could be given to the employer.

Resumes. Extra copies of the resume can be provided to selection committee members or other individuals involved in the interview process who may not have had a chance to review the resume submitted with your application.

Teaching Certificate. A copy of the teaching certificate can clarify questions regarding certification or certification probability. The original certificate obtained from the department of public instruction should be photocopied and put away for safe-keeping. If the teaching certificate has not yet been issued, include a list of subject areas in which certification will be granted.

Philosophy Statement. Because interviewers often ask about your philosophy of education, it may be helpful to have developed your ideas in a few carefully-constructed paragraphs. Photocopies of the statement could be given to the interviewer as a supplement to (not as a substitute for) your verbal response.

Sample Lessons or Units. Presenting examples of lesson plans and/or units developed or implemented may emphasize and reinforce a response to an employer's question about previous teaching experience. The materials contained in these samples can illustrate organizational ability as well as knowledge of the subject area and creativity. Teachers in certain fields should routinely have available the following items:

Art majors — slide presentations of your work:
    examples of student projects

Music majors — vocal or instrumental arrangements, marching band patterns, tapes of student performances or lessons

Language majors or
Bilingual teachers — audio tapes involving student participation or
    a bilingual lesson.

Character References. College placement files appropriately contain references related to educational and professional experiences. Character references from ministers, business and political leaders, neighbors, etc. could be included in the portfolio and offered to employers who may express an interest in this type of reference.

Paper and Pen. Make a habit of including these materials in an interview portfolio. If needed, they are immediately accessible without rummaging through pockets or purses.

Any or all of the items suggested can be attractively arranged in a simple manila folder, notebook binder or other hand-designed cover. Organize the material so that it is convenient for presentation during the interview. As you progress in your career, relevant material should be added and out-dated items deleted. The interview portfolio is not only an effective visual tool, but will assist you in organizing materials which will be helpful at various stages of the job search.

INTERVIEW	PORTFOLIO
Transcripts	*Sample Lesson or Unit*
Resumes	*Slides or Tapes*
Teaching Certificate	*Character References*
Philosophy Statement	*Paper, Pen*

Interview readiness involves more than organizing papers related to professional work and qualifications. Mental preparation is a key factor in determining interview success. In anticipation of the interview you have organized your thoughts about yourself and your profession, you have learned as much as you can about the school district and the community, you have reviewed typical interview questions and formulated relevant questions of your own, and you have developed your own mental checklist to ensure that points you consider essential are covered. An important, but often ignored, step in the preparation process, involves practicing for an interview. Practicing can involve role-playing with a friend, audio or video taping to learn more about your vocal/physical mannerisms, or simply practicing with a mirror. Most of us are reluctant to attempt this type of simulation but its value is inestimable. The goal of all interview preparation is to become as familiar and comfortable as possible with interview routines and expectations, so that the interview can be approached in a relaxed and confident manner. Having adequately prepared, you can arrive at the interview with a positive attitude and the ability to make a good impression.

First Impressions Are Lasting Impressions

A favorable first impression, the result of careful and thorough preparation, will have an effect on overall interview performance. First impressions may involve

>   promptness,
>
>   courtesy,
>
>   etiquette,
>
>   grooming.

In most situations, a date and time for the interview have been established. You are expected to be on time but it is far better to be a few minutes early than to arrive late, hurried, and nervous. The few extra minutes will allow you to gather your thoughts and, if necessary, to touch up windblown hair, a crooked tie, etc.

Upon arrival at the interview site, the first person encountered will usually be a secretary or receptionist. State clearly your name, the time of your appointment, and the name of the person you expect to see. You may engage in conversation with the receptionist, but you should not initiate it. Be courteous. The impression you make on the receptionist will not get you a job; it may, however, cost you one.

A knowledge of basic interviewing etiquette will assist in making a good first impression. As a general rule, let the interviewer initiate a handshake, but be prepared so that there is no fumbling to free the right hand. After the introductions are completed, wait for the interviewer to offer a visual or verbal invitation to be seated. In most situations, it will be to your advantage to refrain from smoking even if invited to do so. It will always be wise to refrain from chewing gum.

Dress and personal grooming can play an important role in the interview process. Appropriate interview attire is essential. It is better to be slightly more on the conservative side than to adopt the latest fad. Your overall appearance, including clothing, shoes, accessories, and jewelry, should be appropriate to a professional.

INTERVIEW PREPARATION CHECKLIST			
YES	NO		
[ ]	[ ]		Am I knowledgeable about the school district?
[ ]	[ ]		Am I informed about the community?
[ ]	[ ]		Have I organized interview materials?
[ ]	[ ]		Am I aware of the different types of interviews?
[ ]	[ ]		Have I anticipated interview questions?
[ ]	[ ]		Have I formulated questions of my own?
[ ]	[ ]		Have I planned responses to questions which could be discriminatory?
[ ]	[ ]		Do I have an interview plan (mental checklist)?
[ ]	[ ]		Have I practiced being interviewed?
[ ]	[ ]		Have I prepared to make a good first impression?

Interview Closure

Whether the interview lasts for thirty minutes or several hours, be perceptive to signs that the interview is drawing to a conclusion. Do not prolong the interview, but be sure that you know the time line for the selection process as well as any further procedures or supporting documents required of you. Discreetly thank the interviewer for the time and consideration extended, smile, and show as much confidence in leaving the interview situation as you did at the beginning. One way to conclude might be, "If you have any other questions, I hope you will be in touch with me."

Chapter Five: Interviews

Evaluation and Follow-up

No interview is complete without your evaluation. No matter how you feel about the interviewer and the interview, resist the temptation to evaluate the outcome. Your immediate "gut reaction" may not be reliable; don't try to second guess the interviewer about your chances of being offered the position. You should only be in the business of evaluating yourself. You simply do not have the information necessary to make a prediction – you are not aware of the qualifications of the other candidates, nor can you know all the inside information available to the administrator. Concentrate, instead, on evaluating your performance.

It is natural to feel relief after an interview – especially after your *first* professional interview. It is also natural to feel a post-interview let-down. You've been tense and nervous anticipating the interview, and you can expect a temporary slump. Don't be too harsh on yourself. Try to reflect on your performance with some objectivity. Maybe it would be a good idea to begin the process of evaluating your performance by listing the things that you felt good about. At some point you will also want to give some thought to areas in which you might improve your performance. Try to analyze what it was that made you uncomfortable and develop ways of coping with similar situations should they arise in future interviews. Do not dwell on your weaknesses. Concentrate on your strengths and on concrete means of improving problem areas.

For example, you may feel that you talked too much. You may have found yourself elaborating needlessly or rehashing an idea because the interviewer did not immediately show approval or ask another question. In future interviews, you can anticipate this possible problem and take steps to overcome it. Do not be afraid of momentary silences. If you have finished your thought, wait for the interviewer to make the next move. If, after a few seconds, you feel that the interviewer is testing you by silence, you may force a response by asking a question such as, "Is there something more I can tell you about that experience?" Used sparingly, this technique may break some uncomfortable silent moments during an interview.

Once you have evaluated your interview performance and have given some positive thought to future opportunities, it is also to your advantage to evaluate the community. This is especially true if the community is unfamiliar; do not assume a greater familiarity than you really have. Quick impressions from vacations or occasional visits are not sufficient for making the decision to live and work in a particular community. You can make a more reliable judgment by developing and using a community review form similar to the one below.

COMMUNITY REVIEW
NEEDS AND EXPECTATIONS

	Positive +	*Neutral* o	*Negative* —

PERSONAL/FAMILY

Housing	[ ]	[ ]	[ ]
	[ ]	[ ]	[ ]
Lifestyle	[ ]	[ ]	[ ]
	[ ]	[ ]	[ ]
Spouse Employment	[ ]	[ ]	[ ]
	[ ]	[ ]	[ ]
Childcare	[ ]	[ ]	[ ]
	[ ]	[ ]	[ ]
Health Services	[ ]	[ ]	[ ]
	[ ]	[ ]	[ ]
Consumer Goods	[ ]	[ ]	[ ]
	[ ]	[ ]	[ ]

PROFESSIONAL/SOCIAL

Continuing Education	[ ]	[ ]	[ ]
	[ ]	[ ]	[ ]
Organizations	[ ]	[ ]	[ ]
	[ ]	[ ]	[ ]
Affiliations	[ ]	[ ]	[ ]
	[ ]	[ ]	[ ]

Chapter Five: Interviews

Community Review: Needs and Expectations – *Continued*

	Positive +	*Neutral* o	*Negative* –
COMMUNITY			
Attitude	[ ]	[ ]	[ ]
....	[ ]	[ ]	[ ]
Economic Base	[ ]	[ ]	[ ]
....	[ ]	[ ]	[ ]
Environmental Quality	[ ]	[ ]	[ ]
....	[ ]	[ ]	[ ]
Public Transit	[ ]	[ ]	[ ]
....	[ ]	[ ]	[ ]
Commuting	[ ]	[ ]	[ ]
....	[ ]	[ ]	[ ]
Leisure	[ ]	[ ]	[ ]
....	[ ]	[ ]	[ ]
Entertainment	[ ]	[ ]	[ ]
....	[ ]	[ ]	[ ]

Chapter Six

CONTRACTS

A contract is a formal agreement between two parties defining mutual obligations and responsibilities, usually for a specified period of time. Simply stated, a teacher's contract provides that the teacher agrees to exchange certain services (instruction of students in an assigned discipline or grade level) for compensation (salary and other benefits). The contract is designed for the mutual protection and benefit of the two parties — the teacher and the board of education, a representative body elected by the citizens of the district and charged with the responsibility for governing the local public schools.

In most school districts, a master contract is prepared as the result of negotiations between teachers or their bargaining agent and the board of education. The negotiated master contract includes such features as base salary and specified increments, fringe benefits including retirement and insurance plans, number of working days, policies regarding leaves (illness, emergency, and sabbatical), procedures for observation and evaluation, and guidelines regarding termination of services. Because the contract is offered for a specified time period, it may be renewed if such renewal is mutually agreeable. Either party has the option not to renew the contract.

Types of Contracts

There are two basic types of written contracts — comprehensive and supplemental. A comprehensive contract specifies all duties agreed upon by the two parties. Teaching assignments as well as extracurricular responsibilities such as coaching or sponsorship of activities are delineated. Some districts have negotiated a master contract which applies only to teaching responsibilities. Extracurricular assignments or other duties are covered in a separate document referred to as a supplemental or special services contract. The principal advantage of a supplemental contract is that it provides greater flexibility for the district as well as for the individual teacher.

The following sample contracts represent typical agreements between a teacher and a board of education for regular and special services. The language of some contracts can be considerably more complex, but the provisions are generally similar to those outlined in the samples.

Chapter Six: Contracts

POLK COUNTY SCHOOL DISTRICT
In the County of Polk, State of Wyoming

TEACHER EMPLOYMENT CONTRACT

THIS CONTRACT entered into this _____ day of _____, 19___ by and between the POLK COUNTY SCHOOL DISTRICT of Balsam, Wyoming, hereinafter referred to as the District and _____
hereinafter referred to as the Employee —

WITNESSETH

That the District hereby employs the Employee to serve in the public schools of Balsam, Wyoming, for a period of _____ working days commencing on _____, and ending on _____.

In consideration of the services of the Employee as set forth below, the District agrees to pay a salary of $ _____ per school year, payable in twelve monthly installments or, at the employee's option, the last three monthly installments may be paid in one lump sum. The final installment(s) shall not be paid until all reports are complete, filed and approved by the Superintendent or the Superintendent's designee at the close of the school year. Deductible absences shall be computed at the rate of _____ of the annual salary for each day of such absence.

All regulations and policies of the Board of Education relating to the employment and assignment description of teachers, their professional qualifications, Rules of the State Department of Education, and provisions of the negotiated agreement entered into between Polk County Education Association and the Board of Education of the Polk County School District as now adopted, are included herein and become a part of this Contract as if fully set forth.

THE EMPLOYEE further agrees to the following:

1. To register a valid certificate issued by the State Department of Education with the Polk County School District Superintendent of Schools before accepting payment of any part of annual salary.

2. That the employee is not at this date under contract with any other school district, and that the district in entering into this contract does not violate Section 186.9 of the Wyoming School Law.

3. In accordance with State Law 2.1 (11.12) submit to the District's Superintendent of Schools a written medical report of a physical examination by a licensed physician who has performed said examination.

IN WITNESS WHEREOF, the parties have signed this instrument in duplicate.

_____   _____, 19_____
Employee

POLK COUNTY SCHOOL DISTRICT

_____   _____, 19_____
President, Board of Education

POLK COUNTY SCHOOL DISTRICT
In the County of Polk, State of Wyoming

SPECIAL SERVICE CONTRACT

THIS CONTRACT entered into this _____ day of _____, 19___ by and between the POLK COUNTY SCHOOL DISTRICT of Balsam, Wyoming, hereinafter referred to as the District and _____
hereinafter referred to as the Employee —

WITNESSETH

That the District hereby employs the Employee to perform the special services as _____
_____ in the public schools of Balsam, Wyoming, for the term of this contract, commencing on _____, 19___ and ending on _____, 19___.

In consideration of the services of the Employee the District will pay the Employee in addition to the Teacher Employment Contract the sum of $_____ and which payments will be included with the regular Teacher Employment Contract salary payment and subject to appropriate provisions for withholding and deductions.

All regulations and policies of the Board of Education relating to the employment and assignment descriptions of teachers, their professional qualifications, Rules of the State Department of Education, and provisions of the negotiated agreement entered into between the Polk County Education Association and the Board of Education of the Polk County School District as now adopted, are included herein and become a part of this Contract as if fully set forth.

THE EMPLOYEE further agrees to the following:

1. The employee be also employed under a validly executed Teacher Employment Contract during the term covered by this Special Service Contract.

2. This Special Service Contract for services to be performed by the employee in addition to and not as part of the services to be performed by the employee under the employee's regular Teacher Employment Contract.

3. The Board of Education of the Polk County School District shall be the judge of the competence and qualifications of the employee. Failure on the part of the employee to perform adequately the special services as set forth in this Contract shall be deemed to be sufficient cause for cancellation of the Special Service Contract by the Board of Education.

IN WITNESS WHEREOF, the parties have signed this instrument in duplicate.

_____   _____, 19____
      Employee

POLK COUNTY SCHOOL DISTRICT

_____   _____, 19____
    President, Board of Education

There are three basic steps in the contract process. First, the contract is offered to the individual selected by the hiring official or committee. The offer may be verbal or written, and a time-line for the return of the contract will be indicated. The second step involves the candidate's decision to accept or decline the contract. The decision must be communicated to the hiring official within the specified time, either verbally or in writing. It is important to realize that a verbal acceptance may be legally binding and is always ethically binding. After the candidate has signed and returned the contract, it must be signed and approved by the board of education before it becomes official.

Breaking a Contract

A note of caution. Once you have signed and returned the contract to the board of education you are legally committed to fulfill the obligations of the contract and *you are not free to accept another offer.* Do not make the mistake of signing two contracts; you may end up empty-handed. The consequences of breaking a contract can be severe. The board of education has the option to take legal action which could result in the revocation of your teaching certificate by the state department of public instruction.

While a contract must never be broken, it is possible that a teacher might find it necessary to request a release from contractual obligations. Legitimate reasons for requesting a contract release might include:

Spouse transfer. A spouse's unanticipated promotion or career shift can create unavoidable conflicts for a teacher who may have signed a contract with every intention of honoring it. Because people in the business world are sometimes transferred to a new location without extensive prior notice, it is not uncommon for a teacher to seek an immediate or early release from a contract.

Health reasons or family responsibilities Accident or illness can make it impossible for a teacher to fulfill contract obligations. Similarly, unexpected changes in responsibilities for spouse, children, or parent may occur.

Personal reasons. This term may be applied to a variety of situations. A teacher may request a release for "personal reasons" due to extreme job dissatisfaction, personality conflicts, or pre-employment misconceptions. Request for release under any of these circumstances might be legitimate but should only be made as a last resort after careful deliberation and consultation.

Career change. If an opportunity for a new career arises during the term of a teacher's contract and the starting date is not negotiable, the teacher may have no recourse but to request a release.

Job offer from another school district. This situation can arise in two different ways. A more desirable offer may be received just after a teacher has signed a contract for the coming year, or a teacher who is currently under contract may wish to search for a more desirable teaching assignment or location. The board's reaction to a request for release under these circumstances may depend upon when the contract was signed, the time of year the request for release is made, and the availability of satisfactory replacements.

Whatever the teacher's legitimate reason for requesting a release from a contract, most boards of education will make every effort to accommodate such a request. The release may, however, depend upon the availability of a replacement. The board is under no obligation to release a teacher from the terms of the contract; therefore, a contract should never be signed with the expectation of obtaining a release. Contract releases are not automatic. Unless the teacher has the intention of honoring the contract, it should not be signed.

Looking Ahead

With the signing of the contract, your job search is complete. You have found the teaching job that is right for you and you should be looking forward to an exciting and rewarding professional experience. The job-seeking tools and skills you have developed and utilized will guide you throughout your career. Your mastery of the paper tools and personal skills will make it possible for you to make future career decisions logically and wisely. Although you will continue to grow and develop and your goals may change to reflect your experiences and interests, the processes of job seeking will remain basically the same. You can approach any future job search with confidence in your ability to use the tools and skills required so that you will again find the right job for you.

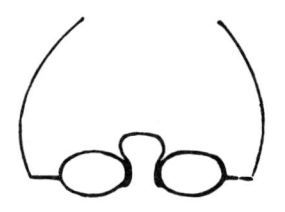

Appendix

XYZABC

BIBLIOGRAPHY

Career Resource Directory, 1982
    by Gerald Roe and Rebecca Anthony
    Association for School, College and University Staffing
    Box 4411
    Madison, Wisconsin 53711

Directory for Exceptional Children, biennial
    Porter Sargent Publishers, Inc.
    11 Beacon Street
    Boston, Massachusetts 02108

Directory of Public School Systems in the U.S., annual
    Association for School, College, and University Staffing
    Box 4411
    Madison, Wisconsin 53711

The Handbook of Private Schools, annual
    Porter Sargent Publishers, Inc.
    11 Beacon Street
    Boston, Massachusetts 02108

Lovejoy's Prep and Private School Guide, 1980
    Simon and Schuster
    1230 Avenue of the Americas
    New York, New York 10020

Patterson's American Education, annual
    Educational Directories, Inc.
    P.O. Box 199
    Mount Prospect, Illinois 60056

Peterson's Annual Guide to Independent Secondary Schools, annual
    Peterson's Guides
    P.O. Box 2123
    Princeton, New Jersey 08540

Private Independent Schools, annual
    Bunting and Lyon, Inc.
    238 N. Main Street
    Wallingford, Connecticut 06386

The Perfect Resume, 1981
    by Tom Jackson
    Anchor Press/Doubleday
    Garden City, New York 11530

Requirements for Certification, annual
    by Elizabeth H. Woellner
    The University of Chicago Press
    5801 Ellis Avenue, Station A
    Chicago, Illinois 60637

The Resume Workbook: A Personal Career File for Job Applications,
    5th ed., 1978, by Carolyn F. Nutter
    The Carroll Press Publishers
    43 Squantum Street
    Cranston, Rhode Island 02920

Sweaty Palms – The Neglected Art of Being Interviewed, 1978
    by H. Anthony Medley
    Lifetime Learning Publications
    10 Davis Drive
    Belmont, California 94002

Each state prepares an annual directory of public and/or private schools. For information regarding availability and purchase price, contact the appropriate state department of public instruction. See pages 39-42 for addresses.

INDEX

Action words, in resumes, 14
Application, letter of, 28-29
Application form, 43-51
   as screening device, 43
   preparation of, 43, 51
   purpose of, 43
   sample of, 44-48

Board of Education, 70-74

Campus interviews, 59
Certification, 4, 38
   dual, 4
   requirements for, 38
   state offices of, 39-42
Coaching, 4, 5
   qualifications for, 4
Community —
   awareness, 67
   evaluation, 67-69
   priority, 2-4
Contract offer —
   acceptance of, 34
      sample letter, 35
   acknowledgment of, 34
   rejection of, 34
      sample letter, 36
   process, 73
Contracts, 70-74
   breaking of, 73
   comprehensive, 70-71
      sample, 71
   purpose of, 70
   release from, 73-74
   special services, 70
      sample, 72
Cover letter, 32
Curriculum Vitae — *See* Resume

Equal Employment Opportunity, 49
   pre-employment information, 12, 49
      sample form, 50

Extracurricular activities —
   rewards of, 4
   sponsorship, 4-5

First impressions —
   in interviews, 65
   in letters, 23
   in resumes, 8, 9
Flexibility —
   community, 2-4
   extracurricular, 4
   geographic, 2
   subject areas, 4
Follow-up —
   sample letter, 33

Grapevine, 28

Interview, 54-69
   anxiety, 56
   basic issues in, 54-55
   body language in, 55-56
   closure, 66
   employer guidelines for, 55
   evaluation, 67
   image, 55-56
   impressions, 65
   interviewer appraisal form, 57-58
      sample, 58
   non-verbal cues in, 55-56
   on-campus, 59
   on-site, 59
   portfolio, 63-64
   preparation for, 59-62
      checklist, 66
   process, 56-57
   purpose, 54
   questions, 60-62
      applicant, 61
      employer, 60
      irrelevant, 62
      readiness, 62-64

Interview — continued
   screening, 56-57
   selection, 57
   simulations, 64
   structure, 56-57

Job market, 1
Job search, 2
   success in, 2
   geographic flexibility in, 2
   community considerations in, 2-4
      community priority list, 3

Letters, 23-37
   application, 28
      sample letter, 29
   checklist, 37
   contract acceptance, 34
      sample letter, 35
   contract rejection, 34
      sample letter, 36
   cover letters, 32
   effective, qualities of, 23
   follow-up, 32
      sample letter, 33
   inquiry, 30
      sample letter, 31
      timing of, 30
   introduction, 27
   outline, 25
   personalizing of, 26
   purpose, 26, 27, 28, 30, 32
   request, 27
   response, 27, 32
   salutation in, 26
   stationery, 26
   style, 24, 25
   tone, 26

Master contract — *See* Contract

Portfolio —
   for interviews, 63-64

Questions —
   applicant, 61
   discriminatory, 61-62
   employer, 60
   open-ended, 43

Records, 51-53
   organization, 51
   samples, 52-53
      job card, 52
      job log, 53

Resume, 7-22
   action words in, 14
   category headings for, 13
   checklist, 22
   definition of, 7
   essentials for, 9, 10
   graphics, 15
   initial contact, 7, 8
   interviewing, 8
   irrelevant information, 12
   length of, 9
   names for, 7
   novelty, 15
   options for, 10-11
   preparation of, 8-13
   production of, 21
   professional writers of, 15
   samples, 16-20
   suggested words for, 14
   updating and maintaining of, 21
   use of, 7, 8

Teacher Certification — *See* Certification
Thank-you note —
   sample letter, 33
Titles, use of, 26

Vita — *See* Resume